The Independent Thinker:
How to Think for Yourself, Come to Your Own Conclusions, Make Great Decisions, and Never Be Fooled

By Patrick King
Social Interaction and Conversation Coach at
www.PatrickKingConsulting.com

Table of Contents

Introduction _____ 7

   The Levels of Mastering Independent Thought _____ 7

   Independent is not the Same as Contrarian _____ 14

   The Fundamentals of Independent Thought _____ 17

   What independent thinking actually looks like _____ 25

Chapter 1: Freedom from Illusions of Reality _____ 35

   Feelings Aren't Facts _____ 39

   Perspective Isn't Reality _____ 44

   Perception is Biased _____ 49

   Memories are Wrong _____ 62

Chapter 2: Freedom from Internal and External Pressures _____ 71

   Battle Confirmation Bias _____ 78

   Follow the Evidence _____ 84

   Battle Social Influence _____ 92

Chapter 3: Freedom from Flawed Thinking _____ 107

Curious as a Cat _____ 114

A Skeptic's View _____ 122

The Critical Thinker _____ 130

Paul-Elder Thinking _____ 137

The Laws of Logic _____ 156

Chapter 4: Freedom from the Demands of Others _____ *169*

Setting and Enforcing Boundaries ____ 171

Choosing and Enforcing Your Boundaries _____ 175

Toxic Takers _____ 196

Chapter 5: Freedom from Yourself _____ *205*

The Courage to Change _____ 206

The Story-teller vs. the Experiencer __ 208

Perceiving the Real _____ 212

The Stoics, ACT and the Power of Value _____ 217

Taking Control of a New Narrative ___ 226

Summary Guide _____ *233*

Introduction

What does it really mean to be an independent thinker?

In the spirit of originality, let's begin not with the perspective of this book's author, but with *yours*.

When you opened this book, you had a few expectations about what you'd find inside, as well as some idea of why you were reading such a book. These expectations may be unconscious, or you may be more aware of them. But whatever they are, they're an excellent starting point for the themes and ideas we'll be exploring in the chapters that follow.

The Levels of Mastering Independent Thought

In choosing this book, you've already shown a desire for, or interest in, independent thought. Some part of you is already independent. And yet, ironically, in picking up a book that guides and teaches you how to be more independent, you must necessarily already lack this characteristic. If you were truly independent, you would not need the book, right?

Take a moment to imagine in your mind's eye everything you associate with an "independent thinker." Imagine it now, before you read on. Imagine what it looks like, sounds like, and how you envision you'll be once you are a more critical thinker, a more authentic individual and self-governing agent able to live in the integrity of their ideals, instead of other people's.

Now, this somewhat disheartening start is simply to illustrate that many people are merely imitating autonomy in the personal development world. They have a picture of what they think this looks like, and they try their best to perform that image.

Level 1: A patchwork Identity

Maybe in your mind, you're attracted to the "cool guy" aesthetic that certain celebrities, authority figures, historical personages and fictional characters put forward. Maybe you like the attitude of the rebel, who is confident, a little arrogant, and so, so appealing. Maybe, without realizing it, you mimic the mannerisms, beliefs, thoughts, and speech patterns of people you admire. Or maybe you buy into certain shared cultural ideals of what intelligent, independent, enterprising or creative people ought to look like.

Teenagers are masters at mimicry and creating patchwork identities from bits and pieces they find in their world. It's as though you show up to the great Identity Marketplace, being a blank slate yourself, and pick and choose the costume and role you like best. It's not a personality so much as a curated collection. While a 13-year-old going through a goth phase in the 90s may be a blatant example of this, we *all* do it to some extent. We even do this when we're explicitly trying not to do it (i.e., "I want to be a truly unique individual! Now, let's Google some other people who are doing that and see how it's done...").

This is the first level on the path of independent thinking.

Level 2: Developing trust in the self

If you've been in level 1 for any length of time, you'll notice something obvious: it's uncomfortable, and it doesn't really "work." You don't feel like yourself because you aren't yourself. No matter how compelling and well-crafted the patchwork is, it's still just a mask, and it doesn't contain *you*. Now, this isn't a problem. Humans are social creatures, and imitation is a normal and healthy part of engaging the external world. But eventually, as we develop and mature into our authentic selves, imitation is not enough.

In level 2, you gradually experiment with being and acting in the world *as yourself*, without a mask and the influence of other people. You begin to tire of other people's filters and interpretations and become curious about your own, which you realize are valid. In all honesty, becoming an independent thinker can feel scary, awkward and outright weird. It can also feel lonely, like you are suddenly far away from the warm, comfortable crowd and have to suddenly take full responsibility for your own reality.

So, in this stage, you are experimenting with being more independent, falling back into convention, playing with trial and error to test your perceptions, and developing resilience for being truly autonomous (yes, autonomy is a muscle that needs to be strengthened!). You realize that dependence on the external has its advantages and that it comes with a cost. While it can be intimidating to tune out other people's opinions, culture, society's expectations and so on, it can also be incredibly rewarding to remind yourself of your own sense of right and wrong, your innate feeling of what you want, and your deepest core values.

Level 2 can be tricky, because it's here that we start to encounter our own mindsets, biases and assumptions at a level deeper than their superficial presentation. We realize that we, like everyone else, possess a reality filter. We don't encounter reality, but reality as it appears after it's been pushed through this filter. The filter takes shape according to our past experiences, family history, cultural environment, religion, education, the historical period we live in, and class...

We all take in the same data, but we come to different interpretations of what that data means because of our different perspectives. The question at level 2 is, are the filters working for you? What do you *want* the filters to be? Can you live without filters at all...?

Level 3: Truly independent thought

Follow that line of reasoning long enough, and you start to understand something important: choice. As an individual, you can choose what material you take in, choose how you respond to it, and choose what you wish to create and put out into the world. And in that act of choosing, you express and experience your own perspective, desires, and will. When you choose, you self-create. When you allow others to choose for you, then they create you.

When we are independent thinkers, we have our own weight and gravity, and stand strong in ourselves, regardless of what others are doing or thinking. We are tuned into our inner compass, values, and selfhood. We look within and evaluate actions and ideas according to our own criteria, and not criteria we've borrowed from others or had foisted on us when too young to realize.

We are free, and we are consciously participating in our life rather than passively receiving it, pre-digested by others.

We take responsibility for our worldview and perspective (yes – it's our responsibility to know and maintain the state of being we choose) and engage with the external world with an unshakeable sense of our own dignity and value. We are comfortable testing our own assumptions and the assumptions of others. We don't just think but reflect on our thinking (i.e., metacognition), and we realize that we always have the power to choose our behaviors, thoughts and beliefs. We try to understand things from the inside out rather than happily believing everything we're told. We are no longer an echo of someone else's values or actions or perspectives, but our own original voice.

Sounds great, right?

"Think for yourself" is something people say, but it is an incredibly difficult thing to do. The world is filled with readymade opinions, untested assumptions, unintelligent biases, lazy thinking, denial, escapism, imitation, and unchecked ego. Ask yourself, when was the last time you had a truly independent thought? Something that your own mind generated, and which didn't come directly from more forceful personalities and ideologies around you?

The conventional, unadventurous thinker goes out into the world and asks, "what are the rules of the game here? What am I supposed to be doing?" In this way, he passively asks for the external world to tell him what to value, focus on, feel, and want.

The independent thinker goes out into the same world and instead asks, "what can I create here? What's happening, and how can I learn more about it? What could potentially be? What do I *want to do*?"

There is only one way to think and be for conventional thinkers, and they figure that out by looking outside themselves: other people's opinions, culture, politics, whatever. But to think independently, you need to turn within and generate your own original response, your own authentic perspective and your own view on life. This is infinitely more valuable than anything you've simply been told, because you value *yourself*, and you trust what you know, and what you're capable of.

It's a guarantee that almost all the content you encounter out there in the world is, essentially, telling you what to do, think, feel, or focus on. News headlines, social media noise, junk on the TV, advertising pasted on every square inch of your life, peer pressure, endless political squabbling... You just drift along and go with it without your own independent thought. But the next time you see a talking head on a pixelated screen, realize that **you have a choice**. You can become conscious in that moment and ask yourself, "this is what this person is creating. That's *them*. But what do I think? What do I want to create?"

Independent is not the Same as Contrarian

When I was a teenager and just becoming aware of the possibility of independent thinking, I got into the habit of mistaking cynicism and distrust for critical thinking. I had correctly learnt that the media often lied, and so every time someone mentioned a news article, I would say something like, "come on, you don't honestly believe everything you read, right?"

This annoying habit had come from the unconscious belief that if I wanted to stand apart and be independent, all I had to do was push against the popular opinion. I would never have admitted it at the time, but I assumed that intelligent, switched-on people were necessarily argumentative and oppositional. However, I was a contrarian, and not a truly independent thinker.

What's the difference?

The clue is in the name: a contrarian is contrary to, or against something. You know the bratty two-year-old who will tell you the sky isn't blue just because you said it is? This is the position that has, as its essence, the fact that it's *not* some other position, but that's all it is. It's the "anti" position.

However, an independent thinker forms their opinions and ideas from scratch, not merely in opposition. They do not care about what they disagree with or dislike. For them, critical thinking is not a competition with a winner or a loser. Something within them guides the formation of their opinions – their own experience, logic, reasoning, desires and values. Sure, the outcome is often at odds with convention. But being at odds is not the goal.

There's usually a hearty dose of emotional bias, excitement, passion, or ego driving their resistance for a contrarian. For independent thinkers, though, the thought process is less flashy, more reason-driven, and, well, not as glamorous! Meanwhile, for contrarians, the goal may be to bolster a certain ego-image, or it may be a deeply unconscious psychological need to dominate, to be heard, to stand out, or to protect against assumed attack.

The focus and direction of such thinking is external – it pushes against other people and attempts to certainly affect other people. Some find them fun and interesting and creative and brave, while others find them annoying and get tangled in arguments with them. But for independent thinkers, other people are... beside the point. The goal is to understand. To figure things out. What other people think? Largely irrelevant.

Now, contrarians and independent thinkers often arrive at the same conclusions, but the question is *why* they end up there. They'll often do the same actions (for example, "question everything") but for very different reasons. Often, a genuinely independent thinker will win the admiration of others, who then attempt to mimic that person (see level 1 above) and attach themselves to that worldview to be contrarian. But the independent thinker does not consider the popularity of his position as an indication of its value – he isn't interested in fame, but he also doesn't relish notoriety!

The Fundamentals of Independent Thought

Let's look at ways to develop autonomous, critical thinking in ourselves. Independent thinking is not a personality trait or fixed behaviors but a continually refined attitude expressed in habits.

Habit 1: Critical reading

To practice and strengthen your ability to generate your own opinion, you need to take in information from various sources and engage with it. Passive reading merely absorbs the content with no individual response. But critical reading is where you practice passing the material through your filters, turn it over in your mind, and examine it on many levels. There are two ways to read:

Reading the words (i.e., comprehending the surface level meaning being conveyed), and

Reading beyond the words (i.e., not automatically assuming the words are a perfect and truthful representation of reality, and becoming curious about how and why the words have been written as they have).

For example, you may read a popular current events magazine piece about the dazzling new frontiers of cryptocurrencies and how tech empires are being built to reshape the digital world. If you are just reading the words, you merely try to comprehend and absorb the material as it's given. You assume the excitement and optimism in the piece is natural and obvious, and the author's opinion is an objective reflection that this topic is exciting. At the end of the piece, you think what the author thinks.

Or you could read the words, and also read what isn't written:

What is fact, and what is just presented as fact? What are the assumptions the author is making?

In what ways is the reader being led, convicted or even manipulated?

Why was this piece published and not literally any other piece?

Who is this author, and what is their incentive – economically, psychologically or culturally?

Who benefits from you reading this article and going along with its premise?

What is the evidence for the view being put forward?

*Independent of what the author thinks, what do **you** think about this topic?*

You could read to find out what other people's opinions are so that you can have them too. Or you can read to gather information, analyze it, and use it to inform your own position. It's a mistake to think that "critical reading" means exposing yourself only to that material you already like and agree with. But an independent thinker is not threatened by low-quality or challenging information – because they trust their ability to appraise and evaluate whatever is in front of them.

Habit 2: Not getting too fond of your own perspective

Don't be the person who finds their position and then clings onto it forever after, no matter what. Humans have a natural bias for protecting and defending the opinions they already hold. They naturally seek information that confirms these opinions, and work hard to discount everything that directly challenges it.

To be an independent thinker, you need to get into the habit of poking holes in these cherished opinions. Now, this is not a cognitive or intellectual exercise. It's a psychological one. Most people have ample brain power to see the plain truth. However, even ultra-intelligent people jeopardize themselves when allowing bias, ego and fear to control them.

Getting too attached to your perspective means you don't abandon it when you should – i.e., when confronted with ample evidence that something is rubbish. Many people like to style themselves as smart philosopher types yet only seem to invoke their vast intellectual powers to reinforce sloppy beliefs and opinions they formed without a second thought. Be independent of other people's opinions, but free yourself from the chains of your own outdated opinions, too. This takes two things: humility and curiosity.

Thinking novel, original thoughts means we have to go outside our comfort zone. The biggest threat to generating a truly unique and new idea is the assumption that you have the best idea already! Independent thinkers can think outside themselves and try different worldviews for size.

They genuinely want to see the world through the eyes of people different from them. That means that they don't engage others to argue or win them over but to actively expand their own understanding. They don't read new material, get into conversations about the idea that they need to defend themselves, or forcefully make their point until the other person recognizes them as the winner!

Habit 3: Being OK with being disliked

Independent thinking means thinking that is *not dependent.* But, dependent on what? The thoughts, opinions, reactions or behavior of others.

So, you think what you think even if other people don't agree, don't understand, or actively don't like you because of it. It comes down to how you view the *purpose* of thinking:

For conventional thinkers, an opinion or thought is an identity marker, or a stick to beat others with. It's something done to win other people's approval or comply with norms and fashions. They engage at the superficial level, i.e., within the realm of other people's thoughts about reality.

For independent thinkers, the primary goal is always to learn, understand, and *directly* engage with reality. Therefore, having their thoughts and opinions disliked is not a problem.

It's far more satisfying to be respected than to be liked. Being the same as people around you can outwardly make you feel safe and accepted. Isn't it better to witness and appreciate the differences in one another and still respect them and cooperate, not in spite of differences, but because of them?

Mature adults can disagree without it threatening their relationship or causing trouble. They also don't expect everyone else to be identical to them as a condition of their friendship or affection. They enjoy and relish challenges and differences. They like the friction and find it useful and generative. A group where everyone thinks the same is not experiencing true harmony and closeness; rather, they have all merely agreed to mimic one another in non-threatening ways.

There is one big difference between the contrarian thinker and the independent one: the ego.

For the former, the most important is the ego, and their way of thinking and being in the world is present to serve that. Meanwhile, the most important thing is genuine insight, understanding, creativity, and mastery for the latter. If the selfish ego hinders that, then that ego is dropped, every time.

Habit 4: Always staying curious

The ego wants to *have* all the answers, like a precious possession to be hoarded and guarded from others. Conventional thinkers prefer the feeling of being seen to be right than they do actually being right. One final habit that sets independent thinkers apart is their commitment to curiosity, instead of clinging to assumed "facts" and never questioning them.

Genuinely questioning the world is a lot harder than it looks. How many of us assume that if someone quotes a scientific paper in their argument, this is automatically sound and has to be accepted? How many of us see statistics and assume that it is correct – because numbers are more trustworthy than words, right? How many of us believe that if a PhD expert in their field says something, it must be true?

Well, this information may be true. But if it is true, it's not *because* it was in the right publication, or written by the right author, using the right terminology. It's true because we could find enough sound evidence to support the fact. This is a subtle but major distinction. As independent thinkers, we question everything, including the ingrained and culturally sanctioned methods of questioning what others have taught us!

You are most at risk for sloppy and useless thinking when you are most blind to your own shortcuts, assumptions, prejudices or expectations. It's great to challenge all the biases you're already familiar with, but what about all those biases currently invisible to you? How are you going to uncover *them*?

Independent thinkers are driven not by the desire to conform and win everyone's approval, but they are also not reacting defiantly by being automatic rebels. Instead, they care most about real, valuable ideas, thoughts they generate themselves, and using that power of thought to its maximum potential. Independent thinkers are driven by a passion far greater and more lasting than the compulsion to aggrandize the self – they want to improve in life, learn, grow, and bring illumination and understanding to the world in general. It's a much bigger prize, isn't it?

What independent thinking actually looks like

At this point, let's clarify a few characteristics of the independent thinker:

- They can gain awareness of their own thinking *as thinking*, and take conscious control over it rather than passively and unconsciously going along with others.

- They trust their own perceptions, will, desires and interpretations and do not automatically privilege other people's over their own.

- They are comfortable going outside their comfort zone, and don't mind admitting errors or being disliked for their positions.

- They take in enormous amounts of information but actively engage with it, not just on a superficial level but also critically.

- They know their cognitive biases, expectations, blind spots, and the ever-present ego and try to minimize any disturbance to their genuine understanding.

A conventional thinker occupies a mental model unconsciously, and the model they use may be something of someone else's creation. An independent thinker knows many mental models, and owns their responsibility to **choose** which one to occupy, and for what reasons.

This section will look at a few key historical figures who are broadly considered to embody the above characteristics. These thinkers and theorists have demonstrated thoughts and opinions so genuinely novel and independent, that they always have changed the course of history or else drastically broadened the existing paradigm. But in reading about these people, we are not trying to answer the question, "how can I be more like them?" That is simply level 1 thinking! Instead, we want to see what we can learn from their experience, and understand what it says about our *own*.

You may wonder if independent thinkers are always philosophers and scientists. Independent thinking can manifest as the scientific method, but this is not all it is. Seeking evidence, establishing the truth through experiment and falsifiability, and using reason and logic are all used in the sciences, but they are more rightly a part of a broader approach to reality. You need not be a scientist to be an independent thinker! As long as you are questing for deeper understanding and will consider your role in the equation, so to speak, then you are a critical and independent thinker.

The people we'll discuss below all liberally used analytical, logical, conscious, and reflexive mental models. These models gave them a richer and more lively perspective on reality than people who merely swallowed convention without a second thought. You could argue that independent thinking should just be called... thinking. Everything else is a knee-jerk reaction, habit, ego, coping mechanism or piece of culture.

Let's see what we can learn from the independent thinking heavyweights.

Socrates – teaches us about challenging assumptions

Socrates was basically a one-trick pony. That trick? Asking questions. That's it. Socrates wanted to understand. He wanted to dig dep, and when he thought he found an answer, he questioned *that*. He knew that correctly honed mental faculties were humanity's saving grace, and he took it as his mission to use dialogue, logic and reason to uncover the truth.

Besides Socrates' philosophy, he was known for what's now called Socratic dialogue. Reality is revealed to us when we engage with our ignorance. In curiosity, we ask questions, and keep on asking them. We question even our questions, and our means of interpreting the answers. We start from the bare bones, assume nothing, and take small logical steps to discover what we absolutely can know. Socrates would demonstrate this dialectic to uncover hidden assumptions in a literal conversation. Step by step, the Truth is revealed.

In classical Socratic dialogues, two people discuss higher concepts like virtue, the nature of knowledge, and art. But we can use a similar approach to uncover assumptions in our everyday lives. We can ask questions such as:

"What do I mean by XYZ?" (what assumptions have I made about definitions?)

"What is my evidence for thinking this?" (do I have any reason to believe it?)

"What do I know here?" (and what am I simply guessing?)

"What am I (or you) not seeing?" (I may have made an error by omission)

Getting a handle on your own assumptions means being willing to think from scratch. Consider even what you think is obvious and ask, is it really that obvious? Is it a given? You might ask yourself a series of the above questions five times in a row to get to the root of your deepest held assumptions. This process might not illuminate the truth, but it will show you more clearly any impediments to seeing that truth!

"I think I've got cancer."

Is that so?

"Well, I've got this weird lump, and I know what that means... cancer!"

Does a lump always mean you have cancer?

"Well, I don't know. But I've read that it's a big warning sign."

Is what you read absolute proof that you have cancer right now?

"Well, no, obviously not. But I could."

What is the evidence?

"There's no evidence exactly..."

So, what do you *really* know?

"Uh. I guess the only thing I really know is that I have a lump."

Niall Ferguson – teaches us the power of counterfactual thinking

Famously a historian who wrote about alternative history (specifically, what life would have been like if Germany had won World War II), author Niall Ferguson was a master of using the all-powerful phrase, *what if?* Counterfactual thinking is an out-the-box approach that is intrinsically innovative and creative. Every independent thinker must be familiar with the process of seeing what is… and being curious about what isn't.

For example, in business, you could use counterfactual thinking to look at past failures and imagine how things could have played out differently, thus devising an improved strategy that prevents those mistakes in future. If you've asked a question and gotten a puzzling answer, it's counterfactual thinking that helps you imagine what the right question would look like.

This thinking style is a little strange and unfamiliar to those used to working only with what's right in front of them. Still, for those natural inventors and creatives of the world, thinking about what could be is as important as thinking about what is. When you ask *what if*, you step out of your comfort zone, drop all assumptions and pet theories, and take a leap into the possible, potential, and theoretical. This is where novel solutions are found, new ideas are explored, and fresh views are taken on old situations. In a way, Socrates was also a counterfactual thinker in the sense that he repeatedly asked, "what if everything I think I know is actually wrong? What then?"

Friedrich Nietzsche – teaches us about perspective

Nietzsche was a philosopher who knew how much ego stood in the way of understanding, and he made liberal use of teasing, criticism and humor to poke holes in the prevailing yet unexamined ideologies of the time. Rather than being a nihilist, Nietzsche was instead keenly aware of the fact that every person inhabits a particularly conditioned perspective, informed by where they're born, when, how they're educated, who their parents are and what their culture teaches them.

Unaware of their impact, we are slaves to these influences. But if we become aware of our circumstances, we give ourselves choice. We master ourselves and the world at large, and become the creators of our experience rather than at its mercy. Nietzsche believed that one way to get outside of these perspectives was to liberally try on as many as possible, and genuinely see the world through other people's lenses.

Nietzsche said, "There is only a perspective seeing, only a perspective "knowing"; and the more affects we allow to speak about one thing, the more eyes, different eyes, we can use to observe one thing, the more complete will our "concept" of this thing, our "objectivity," be." Thus, all there is in the world for us as human beings are different subjective perspectives of that world. But if we can appreciate as many perspectives as possible, we gain a richer and more intelligent view of that world. For Nietzsche, there are no facts, only interpretations, and every person adopts their worldview and mental models to serve their needs. Our egoism is merely a narrowing of perspective; to free ourselves as much as possible, we need to widen that perspective and mix it up.

One great way to do this: find a point of view that is diametrically opposed to your own, and pretend it *is* your own. Make arguments for it. Imagine that, in its way, it makes complete and perfect sense. Genuinely engage with people who disagree with you – imagine that in doing so, you are accessing another aspect of the issue that you were previously blind to. Your world becomes bigger.

Summary:

- Independent thinkers can think logically, clearly and autonomously, outside the pressures of their cultures, upbringings, past experiences or historical period. They are conscious and aware, rather than reactive and automatic, and can truly think (and experience) for themselves.
- Cultivating independent thought takes time and effort. The first stage is to assemble a patchwork identity as an independent thinker, and mimic others we see around us. The second stage is to gradually develop trust in our own perceptions and intellectual faculties, while occasionally deferring to convention. The final step is truly independent thought. This free, adventurous, creative, and proactive thought originates purely within us.
- The fundamentals of critical thought include learning to take in information (especially reading) critically, dropping the ego so that you don't get stuck in any one perspective or opinion, having the bravery to be disliked for being different, and maintaining an open and receptive rather than closed mind. Conventional thinkers differ from independent thinkers in their approach to reality itself, and how they see the function of thinking. For the former, it's to bolster the ego. For the latter, it's for the thrill of encountering reality directly.

- Independent thinking is a way of being that can be practiced and nurtured. We do this by cultivating awareness, dropping ego, and learning to engage critically with the information we take in. This is not the same thing as being a contrarian, who goes against the grain merely to rebel.
- Many famous independent thinkers throughout history shed light on how we might develop the capacity in ourselves. Socrates teaches us the power of asking questions and uncovering our assumptions by taking nothing for granted. Niall Ferguson teaches us about counterfactual thinking, and imagining answers to the question "what if?", and Nietzsche teaches us the value of perspective-switching to enrich our perception of the world.

Chapter 1: Freedom from Illusions of Reality

We've had a brief look at what independent thought is and looks like, as well as the different stages or levels of its development as we mature as autonomous thinkers. Let's dig a little deeper now and consider one not-so-obvious way to immediately improve our intellectual faculties: remove the biggest obstacles that stand in their way.

In the chapters that follow, we'll consider the major impediments to truly independent thinking and remove them one by one, almost as though we were gradually polishing a mirror, removing layer after layer of grime and dirt. Once the mirror (i.e., our powers for independent, rational thought) is spotless, we can see reality in crisp and perfect clarity.

The biggest threats to robust and clear thinking lie within us. As mentioned earlier, the biggest mistake we can make when improving our critical thinking skills is to falsely assume that we are thinking at all! An example will demonstrate this perfectly: a big firm hiring team spends countless person-hours and invests tons of money into candidate screening software and complicated interview processes, all in an earnest attempt to hunt out and hire the objectively best new employees. In the final interview round, the boss takes a look at a candidate and announces, "I know her final scores weren't great, but I don't know, I've got a good feeling about her. Let's pick her."

Or perhaps worse, because this candidate unconsciously reminds him of his daughter or because her accent or her shoes or the spelling of her name holds some unconscious positive associations for him, the boss announces that she is, in fact, the best candidate. He genuinely believes this is a rational, obvious choice, and he may convince everyone else that it is, too!

Humans tend to place significant value on *instinct*. Especially as the pace of modern life forces us at times to think quickly on our feet and make immediate decisions, we believe that having superior *instinct* helps us get along. That's certainly true to an extent. Human beings are biological beings inhabiting bodies, and we have evolved like every other animal to make split-second decisions that promote our survival

– decisions that need to be far quicker than our higher-order thinking could ever manage. If you're in a strange new environment and your gut tells you it's dangerous – there's a strong case for following that instinct.

The problem is that sometimes we confuse instinct as a substitute for good judgment. It's a different story when we allow our gut to tell us "this is dangerous" when our conscious mind *knows* it isn't – for example, when fear makes you procrastinate going to the dentist! The error comes in assuming that instinct and gut feelings are always correct or that these hunches are sufficient for helping us make more complex life decisions.

Instinct and good judgment are entirely separate things. They are two separate ways of processing information – both have value, but they need to be used in the appropriate context. For this, you need to consciously be aware of how and when you are employing them respectively. Instinct may sometimes overlap with good judgment, but they are not interchangeable. Let's look at the differences:

Good judgment comes through a process of experience over time, while instinct and hunches are incredibly quick—almost instant. Just as the Grand Canyon was created through an extremely long process, good judgment requires a similar amount of refinement and progress. But with a well-developed sense of judgment, you invariably improve your gut instincts, too. It is possible to have your conscious, rational mind and its powers of judgment working in tandem with your gut instincts, resulting in conscious perception and processing of life that is nuanced, dynamic, and intuitive. In the above example, the boss could become aware of his bias towards the candidate and the objective data and consciously and intelligently weigh these up, coming to a decision that factors in both.

Good judgment is invariably balanced and thorough. Neither of those words describes our base instincts.

Instincts are otherwise known as gut feelings or hunches, and, unless you are the literary detective known as Sherlock Holmes, are probably wrong the vast majority of the time. Instinct by definition is evaluating based on limited information. It turns out that when we make quick decisions based on instinct, we are usually jumping to conclusions and not seeing the whole picture. We already know that humans are predisposed to prefer speed and certainty over accuracy, which is why it's so important to act against what your instincts want to tell you.

In addition to being Sherlock Holmes, unless you have the eye of an eagle, the ears of a rabbit, and the nose of a bloodhound, there's just no way your instinct is going to be correct consistently.

Let's take the field of cooking to illustrate the difference. An experienced chef will be able to use his judgment, based on years of experience, to design a menu that will be versatile and tasty. He will be able to do this time after time through various cuisines. Compare this to the instincts of a neophyte chef. On rare occasions, the neophyte chef's menu might be preferable because there is an overlap between instinct and good judgment. But instinct will fail him in the long run without deeper knowledge.

We are biologically programmed to go with the first thought that pops into our head, a recipe for disaster. This chapter covers how to overcome the traps that come from relying on that initial flood of certainty in many ways, from our emotions, perspectives, perceptions, and even memories. This will involve creating psychological distance from yourself to stop acting against your interests.

Feelings Aren't Facts

One common error that all of us have made at some point in our lives is interpreting our emotional responses as truth—that is, confusing our feelings for facts. We observe or experience a situation that causes certain feelings to stir, and we interpret them not as subjective interpretations but a tangible reality.

This is otherwise known as emotional reasoning, and it is the polar opposite of clear thought. In emotional reasoning, you agree with the following statement: "I feel this way; therefore, it must be true." If you feel negatively about a certain person, they must be terrible people. If you feel optimistic about a test, it must be easy. If you feel doubtful about a promise, the person on the other side of the promise must be scheming something. Emotions, both mild and intense, create an altered reality.

It's often a process that evades our conscious thought, making it tough to spot.

On the one hand, it shouldn't be surprising that emotions can disrupt our thinking so powerfully. Emotions have overlapping purposes with instincts; they are both "act first, analyze later" types of thinking, a phenomenon that has kept us alive as a species. Both emotions and instinct were designed to short circuit our brains and push analytical thought out of the way in favor of action.

While engaging in this behavior, observed evidence is discarded in favor of the truth of your feelings about the event. Emotional reasoning is one of the most dangerous obstacles to clear thought because it can be so wildly different from reality and can change in the span of minutes. Is reality changing moment by moment? Of course not! Only your emotions are changing that quickly.

Just like you wouldn't go grocery shopping when hungry, you shouldn't evaluate anything when emotional. Always take time to return to a calm state before making decisions or committing yourself to a specific course of action.

Reality is neutral, and your emotions cause you to perceive it in any particular way. Viewing a situation with emotional reasoning is like watching a completely benign scene with horror music being repeatedly played. And then joyous music. And then the next minute, music fitting for a clown's entrance. Now compound this with the act that everyone has a different soundtrack playing over the same scene. You won't know what's happening in front of your face because the music will influence you a certain way. The only hope you have is to *turn off the music*—by removing emotions from the equation as best as you can.

Phobias are a prime example of how we confuse facts and feelings. For example, an agoraphobic person fears outside or open places with no immediate escape route. There's no established factual basis for this fear, especially since so many people *aren't* agoraphobic. Sure, bad things *can* happen to someone when they're outside the home, but the huge majority of the time, they don't. But an agoraphobic's fear has irrationally turned itself into a fact in their mind; therefore, they're not leaving the house anytime soon.

Those who interpret feeling as facts have it completely backward. Our emotions are *products* of our thoughts. They are how we decide to interpret what we experience based on the observations and information we've received from the world around us.

I'm not suggesting you *not* have feelings—that's impossible. But you can and should treat your feelings like every other bit of information you receive. It should be *one* factor in how you think and evaluate situations and people. There might be a reason you feel a certain emotion; it might also exist because of entirely unrelated matters. The simple truth is that when we are emotionally invested, we lack the proper perspective to think clearly. Think of it as standing too close to a brick wall such that you can't see the entire building, only a singular brick. You'd need distance to see reality.

Focus on separating your emotional reaction from your actual response. Feel the first emotional reaction and label it as drastic and emotionally influenced. Let it pass or dissipate. Now, begin to dissect it. Only at this point can you think clearly and rationally. Of course, it must be mentioned that this isn't a point on becoming a cold, calculating robot—although, for our purposes of clear thinking, there could be worse things.

This is a point to ensure you aren't being controlled by emotion, which is not based on evidence or what's in front of you—it's based on past experiences, assumptions, or unfair associations. Feel your feelings—sometimes they signal something that you don't consciously perceive, which is why they shouldn't be discounted—but don't become overwhelmed by them. Also, beware that people are triggers for strong emotions, which can distort reality even more than usual.

Perspective Isn't Reality

Now that we've articulated that feelings aren't facts, it's time to discuss another instance where your first impression will lead you astray. It's also another instance that can be characterized as "what you see is *not* what you get."

We can begin with a fable of sorts that you may have heard before. It's the fable of the six blind men and the elephant. These six blind men happened to surround an elephant one day. How they ended up there is unimportant, but if you require a backstory, pretend that they are on a surprise field trip with their scrabble team. Now, elephants are quite large, which means each blind man was situated at a different part of the elephant. One by one, they reached out to the part of the elephant that was nearest to them: the knee, the side, the tusk, the trunk, the ear, and the tail.

What followed was mass confusion. Even though it was one animal, each man had only his sense of touch to discern what he was standing by. From the descriptions they each gave, it was as if they were standing in completely different ecosystems, much less touching a different animal. An elephant ear can feel like a bat's wing, the side can feel like a rhino, the tusk can feel like a building, and the trunk can feel like a tree trunk swaying in the wind. Six different positions yielded six different perspectives.

The thing is, none of these blind men was wrong, but their perspectives were limited by what they could feel in their positions, to the point that they ended up being incredibly wrong about the elephant's overall appearance.

Perspective is not reality, it's just *your* perspective, and you must gain a three-dimensional view of a situation or decision to think clearly about it. Whether you want to admit it or not, we are all some version of the six blind men, only feeling what's in front of us and not being able to conceive of what we might be missing.

For a more direct illustration, just imagine that for two people standing across from each other, the number 6 drawn in chalk at their feet is also a 9 (or is it the other way around?).

There's no right or wrong way to perceive a given situation or object. Our ideas, images and opinions of life are all subject to molding through our experiences. Nobody has a foolproof, 100% objective way to perceive reality accurately. However, there is a *complete* way to view things, and it necessarily involves as many perspectives as possible.

Take a man and a woman walking out of a motel in the middle of the afternoon in slightly disheveled clothes.

Some of us would have zero impression because we are too distracted and busy. A moral crusader might assume that they were having an afternoon fling intended to be kept secret from their significant others. Someone who works in an adult industry might be so desensitized to such a sighting that it barely registers to them at all. Meanwhile, someone who works as a travel agent may not even consider what the couple were doing in their room; they'll wonder how much they paid for the room and what rating they would give it. And the motel housekeeper probably just cares about how much of a mess they're going to clean up.

The point is, we can take a moment as minuscule and unimportant as this one and run with it, making assumptions, predictions, or judgments that may be completely inaccurate, simply because of what we know (or, more accurately, what we *think* we know). We do this based on our character, values or experiences. And it's a natural and nearly unpreventable thing to do. But it's not reality.

Any number of things shape our interpretations of events and situations in the world. Our religious, political or philosophical leanings can shape how we see the world. So can our childhood upbringings. So can drugs or alcohol usage. So can the media. So can our social or institutional environment. So can our fondness for cats or dogs. So can whether we prefer books, movies or television. It can be any influence whether we're aware of it or not.

Individual perspectives can also come from what are known as *schemas* and *heuristics*. They are both psychological concepts that organize what we know about the world and facilitate quick decision-making.

Schemas. A schema is a model by which we arrange and decipher the information we receive. It allows us to say, "Okay, based on these three factors I can observe, I know what this is." Imagine a schema as a snapshot of a certain situation, and using that snapshot to arrange unfamiliar information. A schema will help you understand that you are in a fancy restaurant, based on the tuxedos and golden toilets you see.

Introduced by psychologist Jean Piaget, we have schemas for many situations. Schemas develop throughout our entire lives, though they're at their most prevalent when we're learning about something for the first time. But while schemas are extremely useful, they can steer us toward unwarranted biases or errors. Of course, they are uniquely personal to us, depending on our experiences.

Heuristics. While schemas help (and hurt) us in interpreting new situations, heuristics are more about how you fit into a new situation. "If this is the situation, then I should act in this way." A heuristic will help you know exactly how to act in that fancy restaurant.

We make hundreds of decisions every day. Most are small, ultimately trivial ones: what we'll have for lunch, what radio station we'll listen to on the way home, what grocery store we're going to shop at, and so forth, unlike major life decisions that could have long-term consequences. We simply can't evaluate every last detail or possible ramification about small decisions. It would be a waste of valuable time and mental energy.

That's where heuristics come in. They're mental guidelines based on past experiences to make daily decisions that we can't delve deeply into. Think of heuristics as flashcards: they give us quick, abbreviated information to help us make speedy choices about daily decisions that we can't stop and deliberate over.

Schemas and heuristics take less effort, energy, and time, making everything simple. It forces simplicity upon complex matters, which isn't always helpful; they blind us to the nuanced realities that dwell underneath almost everything under the sun.

Everything in this section culminates in the fact that one can have a million and a half perspectives about anything—but you only start with one of them. To find reality, you need at least a few. You'll need to proactively seek them out, as they won't come naturally.

This is all to say that you seldom have the whole story. Try to see your perspective as one bit of information to evaluate, and then search for the rest of it.

Perception is Biased

Another way we should deviate from our initial instinct is our *perception*.

Perception is similar to perspective, in that they are both about the information you take in from an event or experience. But while perspective is about our experiences and they obstruct clear thinking, perception is about how what you see or hear is interpreted in a way that doesn't represent reality anymore. These are usually known as *cognitive biases*. Perspective has your own unique filter, while perception has your brain's shortcomings' filter on it.

Yet another way in which our brains and instincts fail us? You don't even know half of it!

Cognitive biases are how the brain seeks the path of least resistance and energy preservation. It seeks to jump to conclusions and limit information in the interest of speed over accuracy. It takes what you see and hear, however brief, and assembles a complete story.

You can imagine how this might lead to a lack of clarity of thought. If you want to take the quickest and easiest path to a destination, it means you are going to be missing a whole lot. It's as if the brain handicaps itself and covers one of its eyes to create a picture more quickly by having only half the visual field to process.

And yet, they do have their useful bits. Occasionally that eye patch is beneficial. There are three main instances where this is the case.

When there's too much information to absorb. We live in a time when there's a deluge of facts, data, statistics, stories, accounts—basically too much information. The overload can be exhausting and usually contains at least some bits of info that are of no use to us whatsoever. We can become overwhelmed and paralyzed. So, it becomes necessary to filter out the relevant information and retain only the parts that we can use. This is where schemas and heuristics we discussed earlier come in as well.

Cognitive bias can help reinforce that filter, and it does so in several ways. The brain tends to latch on to the most repeated or recently activated memories. It also tends to remember events or people that are strange or humorous, and notices more strongly when something has changed.

Now, what do we do with that limited amount of notable information? The brain tries to find a story. But, how can you build an accurate story with a beginning, an ending, and a few bits here and there in the middle?

When we need to act quickly. Sometimes, we're in a crunch. Decisions need to be made quickly. If we let ourselves get bogged down by inactivity or don't react swiftly enough, we can fall behind or risk our survival. Cognitive biases can be helpful in that regard—although, again, not without potential hazards.

Cognitive biases cause us to fall back on the most familiar and comfortable things to us. We rely on the most immediate and available resources. We focus on the present situation, preferring to ponder that instead of the past or the future. We concentrate on things we can more easily relate to and eschew tools or assets that don't make much sense. We strongly prefer solutions that look simple, thorough, and relatively risk-free, rather than overly complicated, vague, or unsafe answers.

This may be a perfectly reasonable course of action when the clock's running low. And it's almost entirely fueled by cognitive bias. But since it comes fast and furious, there might be some clean-up you'll have to do once everything's settled down—but perhaps that is not always the most important priority. It's similar to a preference for asking for forgiveness versus asking for permission in the context of doing something you shouldn't be doing.

When we're deciding what we need to remember for the future. The final scene in which cognitive bias might be of assistance concerns memory. If only fragments of our constant information overload are useful to us now, then even less of it will be relevant to us in the days and years to come. So again, we have to cherry-pick the things and details that we remember.

This process involves reduction. We'll discard some of the finer specifics of things and events and form broader, more general memories. We trim some smaller events off and reshape them into a few basic key points. Maybe we'll pick out only a couple of events and elevate them so they represent the whole experience.

In processing these new memories, our cognitive bias again defers to those most meaningful or familiar to the brain. It will also "edit" certain memories, so they become more accessible to us, but specific details might accidentally be removed or inserted in this process, so we remember it slightly differently from how it happened.

Your biased perception can help you on a limited basis, but they are decidedly *not* the path to smarter thinking. Thus, we delve into three of the most prominent biases to understand how to battle them. Remember, they all seek to abbreviate information for easy decision-making and increased retention—not accuracy.

The availability heuristic. The brain tends to prefer information that's most readily available or comes to awareness rapidly. If something simply comes to mind swiftly or is more memorable, we tend to attach an importance to it that it might not really deserve. It excludes supporting information that might be important to consider and countering details that might be used to argue against it.

For example, you might see the topic "tsunamis" trending on Twitter. You follow a couple of links to recent news reports that say tsunamis are expected to happen more often in the near future. The reports are compelling. You feel a little nervous. You become worried that you'll be a tsunami victim. You start thinking that you haven't prepared enough. You get to the point where you think it's inevitable that someday you'll get swallowed up by a tsunami, and there's nothing you can do about it.

In all this concern, you temporarily forget that you live in Kansas, a landlocked state in the middle of the United States where tsunamis never happen. Tsunamis require a large body of water and are best known for small island nations.

That's the availability heuristic in a nutshell: you got spooked by a bunch of instantly accessible information that made you forget the fact that the chances of you getting swept away by a tsunami in Kansas are virtually impossible. When asked about your fears, you answer "tsunamis" and ignore the rash of home burglaries that might be occurring or that you are in danger of losing your job. Just because something is available, or notable does not mean it is important or representative.

Gambler's fallacy. This common cognitive bias magnifies the importance of past events in predicting future outcomes. The bias dictates that conditions and previous results point to the inevitability of something happening down the road—when in reality, each subsequent event is independent of the previous. This bias wants to create a cause-and-effect relationship where none exists. For instance, just because a coin has flipped to the heads side one hundred times in a row doesn't mean that it's more likely for the next flip to be to the tails side. There is no relationship between each flip.

This particular cognitive bias is called the "gambler's fallacy" because it's responsible for many out-of-control gambling addictions. Somebody betting on a football game may say a certain side will win because they've always done so before, or because they've lost so many times that they are due for a win: "The Packers are due a win this week after all the tough losses, and they are going to get it against the Lions!"

Forget that this guy would be a terrible gambler if that's the information he used to lay a bet, but it illustrates the point. The history of the Packers-Lions rivalry doesn't concern how well those teams have played in recent years. The losses of the Packers in recent weeks doesn't mean their turn for a win is coming. *Just because something happened doesn't mean something else will happen.*

Post-purchase rationalization. This cognitive bias seeks to reduce regret based on fairly common consumer behavior.

Say you're shopping for home theatre equipment. You go to a showroom and see a couple different models. One's extremely expensive, features a lot of bells and whistles, and takes up a lot of space. The other's a bit cheaper and smaller, but to the naked ear, doesn't seem to be much different in terms of quality.

You might be persuaded to buy the bigger and more expensive one because it must work better since it's bigger and more expensive. But it puts a serious dent in your bank account and is too big for your living room. And you might not even really be able to tell how well the sound's working.

If you employed post-purchase rationalization, you'd convince yourself that you made the right decision, that it's what you wanted to do all along. You tell yourself that you can indeed hear the difference in sound, and you do indeed need fifteen different plugs and ports. You might know deep down inside that you went overboard, but that knowledge makes you uneasy. Regret makes you feel stupid, and no one likes that. So, you talk yourself into believing that you did the right thing and got exactly what you wanted. No more regret, just eating boxed macaroni and cheese for dinner for the next two months because you spent so much on new speakers.

This type of post-*anything* justifying behavior extends far beyond purchases. Remember clear thinking's biggest enemy, the ego? This is where it returns. We do this sometimes when we defend ourselves from others, but here, we are trying to convince ourselves instead of trying to convince someone else.

So how do we work to improve our perception and avoid being led astray by our shortcutting brain?

Of course, you can start immediately trying to be aware of them in your thinking and note how your perception is likely focused on speed rather than accuracy. But still, that feels inadequate against some of these thought patterns that have been left unchecked our entire lives. A few specific mental exercises can help retrain your thinking to be clear-minded and measured.

Practice thinking of alternative explanations. Instead of making a snap decision, alter your focus to accuracy and not speed. Take your time. Stop feeling anxious just because there is uncertainty or the lack of a clear decision. Don't write the story immediately.

Try to think of multiple reasons or causes. Reserve your judgment and stop jumping to conclusions. For example, if you're sitting in your favorite coffee shop and you notice a huge drop-off in business, you might think it's because the quality of the coffee has declined. But it could also be because more people are making their own espresso drinks, or because it's summer and more people are doing other things outside. Or perhaps the prices the store is charging are keeping people away.

In a sense, this is like reverse storytelling. We often start with the conclusion and try to work backward in life. Instead of filling in all the blanks and identifying only one path to that conclusion, try to work backward and theorize multiple paths.

You might try an exercise of taking a scene, a person, or any other thing, and observing five details or characteristics about it. Then, for each of those details, write down five possible causes that may have led that particular detail to be the way it is. Try to vary the potential causes you list, ranging from the realistic to the downright bizarre. This will train your ability to create a story around every detail, thus giving you twenty-five trains of thought instead of the quickest and easiest for your brain to process.

Most of us think only linearly in terms of cause and effect. But that's ineffective at best to understanding a situation.

Reword your statements as questions. Think of something you consider a declarative, absolute truth. For example: "E-books and e-readers are killing literature." That's a pretty strong statement. But try rephrasing it: "Are e-books and e-readers *really* killing literature?" The mere act of turning it into a question makes your brain start looking for answers. Instead of a conclusion, you've opened up a line of inquiry.

"Well, maybe e-readers are bringing more people to reading—that's good." "They may be changing *how* we read, but they're not really killing how literature is made. Maybe I'm just overly sentimental about physical books." With just that one change to your statement, you've opened up your mind to a new line of inquiry and exploration.

Even the six blind men could have benefitted from this. Instead of the one standing next to the elephant's tail saying, "I am definitely standing next to a willow tree," the situation would have been much improved by asking, "Why does it feel like I am standing by a willow tree?"

Get behind and challenge your assumptions. Let's say you have a very broad belief about poor people: "They're poor because they don't want to work." Challenge that assumption immediately: "Do poor people just not want to work? Or do they have fewer opportunities? They've been closing plants and stores in town for a few years now—maybe they don't have anywhere else to go. And it's hard to get the proper training for a skilled position when you can't afford it... What if there is something else that causes it? What if there are about fifty shades of grey to this matter?" Am I saying something that fundamentally depends on an untested assumption?

The harsh truth is that whatever you think you know about a topic, especially if it involves people's thoughts and motivations, you probably know only about ten percent of what's truly happening.

It's always best to be proactive about challenging your assumptions through self-interrogation, especially through valid news and information sources, including people who really have deep experience in the subject you're thinking of. It's uncertain where many of our assumptions come from, so it's good to reevaluate them from time to time.

Remove your need to be right. The truth is a separate pursuit entirely from this, and sometimes there is a stark contrast because you want to feel a certain way about yourself, especially in front of others. Truth becomes a lot easier to discern when you take your emotional rewards (and punishments) out of the equation and simply try to determine what's *real*.

If you face opposition, it's just going to cause you to dig your heels in and deny, defend, and stonewall. You'll be seduced into caring more about dominating someone than understanding. You'll want to avoid that sour feeling of shame when conceding defeat to someone—anyone. Even if you're right, very few people make friends by saying, "I told you so."

Picture how a desperately stubborn person would act—is that similar to how you act? Could anyone make an honest comparison between the two? Hopefully not.

Even more so, explore being wrong and understand the evoked feelings. Play out scenarios where you are indeed wrong. What feelings will you feel? There may be embarrassment, anger, humiliation, or shame—but do they affect the world or your life? Only if you let them. Perception is only biased if you allow it to remain unchallenged.

Memories are Wrong

More frequently than we would like to admit, we are flat-out wrong about what we think happened in the past. Our memories fail us constantly, but we'd never know because they also rewrite themselves.

Just because our memories are capable of remarkable feats doesn't mean that they aren't subject to just as remarkable errors. A false memory is simply a real memory, which is neurologically identical to a real one, but not based on something that actually happened.

In 1995, Loftus and Coan from the University of California, Irvine, conducted a simple study to investigate how to implant a false memory by fusing it with an existing, real memory. The study involved a subject describing three true memories from his childhood and one false memory. The subject wrote about each of the four memories for five days in a row, summarizing any details or facts he could remember about each of the memories (three real and one false).

Over the five days, the subject began to recall more and more about the false memory, introducing details that were never there, which seemed to stem completely from the subject's imagination. He purported to remember everyone present and even the emotions involved. He was adding onto the false memory, not realizing it was made up.

Weeks later, the subject was asked to rate his memories for how clear they were. He gave a false memory the second highest rating out of the four memories presented. He could provide vivid detail—perhaps because it was fabricated, so the details conformed to his idea of what the experience would usually entail. Memories could be implanted in people just by saying that they had occurred.

If they are not entirely false or fabricated, memories can also be influenced by things as small as suggestive word choice, phrasing, and vocabulary. In 1974, Loftus and Palmer's infamous study at the University of California, Irvine, illustrates this effect.

Subjects watched different videos of car accidents at three different speeds. After, they filled out a survey asking, "About how fast were the cars going when they *smashed* into each other?"

Other groups of subjects watched the same videos and filled out a survey after as well, but the survey instead asked, "About how fast were the cars going when they *bumped/hit/contacted* each other?" The subjects' estimates changed in relation to the verb used, which influenced the perception of speed and impact.

Smashed = 40.8 mph

Bumped = 38.1 mph

Hit = 34 mph

Contacted = 31.8 mph

This simple change in vocabulary affected people's perception of an event, and in essence, changed their memory surrounding it. How reliable can memory truly be when such small variables manipulate us? This was an event that the subjects watched on video—and the speed increased by nearly 10 mph when leading language was used, a discrepancy of 25%.

The ease with which false memories are created is why eyewitness testimony occupies such an ambivalent place in the legal system. Memories can change during interrogation, and sometimes, intentionally. For example, Annelies

Vredeveldt of the University of Amsterdam states that asking questions about a memory can easily take a wrong turn if you ask questions as simple as, "What was the color of his hair?" or "He was a redhead, wasn't he?" The first question assumes that there was a male, and the second question is leading and draws its own conclusions.

Eyewitness accounts are highly trusted by juries, yet highly condemned by judges and attorneys who know better. Researcher Julia Shaw states that to implant a false memory, "you try to get someone to confuse their imagination with their memory and get them to repeatedly picture it happening."

This means repeating a false memory or story to someone can cause them to confuse the false memory with reality, and eventually mesh them with the real account. There is a very thin and blurry line between memory and imagination.

Eyewitness testimony has been questioned since Hugo Munsterberg's seminal 1908 book *On the Witness Stand*. He questioned the reliability of memory and perception, and the legal community has taken notice ever since. What's scary is that research has shown that juries can't tell the difference between false and accurate witness testimony, often simply relying on how confident the eyewitness is (Nicholson, 2014). Additional support for the distrust in eyewitness testimony has been found in analyses by Scheck and Neufel, who proved that eyewitness testimony was frequently present in cases of suspects later exonerated based on DNA evidence.

Christopher French of the University of London sums it up best: "There is currently no way to distinguish, in the absence of independent evidence, whether a particular memory is true or false. *Even memories which are detailed and vivid and held with 100 percent conviction can be completely false."*

Our memories are incredible, but the same malleability that leads to memory feats can also be exploited to show great flaws. The same sponge-like qualities can lead to wrong information and skewed perspectives. These create flawed thinking, not out of unsound logic or perception, but if you remember something to be different from reality, you're going to have some trouble. The main goal of our brains isn't to be accurate or even helpful, and thus, it can be easily manipulated and tricked.

Summary:

- Usually, your brain, instincts, gut feelings, emotions, and hunches are all liars (usually). They aren't doing it on purpose, but they inherently function by jumping to conclusions, saving time, conserving energy, and valuing speed over accuracy. Their goal is to function on less information, and the less of it, the better. Not quite crystal-clear thinking.

- Your feelings and emotions can overpower you and completely color your thinking. But that's confusing feelings for facts. They are entirely separate things. Reality is in fact neutral.

- Your perspective isn't reality. It represents your subjective and unique worldview, but it's not objective, it's not reality, and it is destined to be skewed in terms of your experiences. Some experiences are solidified in what are known as schemas and heuristics, which are the frameworks you use to organize and understand the world.

- Your perception is biased. Understanding the world around you is probably biased because of how the brain jumps to conclusions. These types of jumps are called cognitive biases. They seek to create a story out of as little information as possible, to avoid uncertainty. Battling cognitive biases involves telling stories in reverse, slowing down, and shifting your focus to questions instead of declaratory statements.

- Your memories are wrong. No matter how real and accurate they sometimes feel, a disturbing fact is that memories and false memories end up being indistinguishable to your brain. Factors as small as word choice or pointed questions can distort memories. Unfortunately, we depend on these memories to form our world views and perspectives.

Chapter 2: Freedom from Internal and External Pressures

So, it would seem that our brain's greatest virtue and its biggest limitation are the same: its tendency to create shortcuts, save time, make helpful assumptions and fill in the blanks. We've considered certain quirks and idiosyncrasies of our brains and how we can improve our thinking by being aware of the distortions inherent in our perception, emotions, unique perspectives, and memories. Now let's turn to another major roadblock to independent thought: we can call it a lack of "open-mindedness", or be blunt and call it sheer pig-headedness!

You'd like to think that people place a high value on being open-minded and, as Aristotle said, entertaining multiple thoughts without fixating on one—but sadly, that's far from the reality. It's far from how we are wired as humans. You only have to scroll through the comments of any social media platform or news website to know that people aren't so interested in hearing what other people have to say. If there is a stance, there is an antithesis to that stance. Furthermore, agreeing to disagree is not an option, either. Even when there are no stakes, most people seem to feel tangible, physical pain at the prospect of changing their mind and absorbing conflicting information.

Why are people so closed-minded?

What causes this quirk of humans to hold onto what it knows as the truth, and habitually disregard others? We might like to think that it's only other people who demonstrate this enraging habit, but if we're honest, we are as likely to do it ourselves. Have you ever gotten mad at someone for some perceived slight, geared yourself up to be all indignant and angry about it, only to quickly realize that you were mistaken and that your anger is misplaced? Perhaps you were just about to yell at your roommate for leaving their bike in the hallway only to suddenly realize it's *your* bike in the hallway. You may find that it's quite hard to let go of the initial angry feeling despite intellectually knowing you've made the error. You may still harbor the stubborn opinion that your roommate is inconsiderate and untidy –

the evidence right in front of you seems not to have properly registered. Why? Why do we stick to an opinion—any opinion?

Like many behaviors that emphasize immediacy over accuracy, we can generally use the brain's survival instincts as a scapegoat. It may sound cliché to say at this point, but it's the truth that the human brain is still stuck in the African savannah about 10,000 years ago, and hasn't quite turned down its alarm systems for modern living. Certainty won, while hesitation was hunted down and eaten for dinner.

Being closed-minded is just basic humanity in action. It's not a mistake or glitch; it's an intentional feature of our psyche.

But beyond that, there are plenty of other factors that keep us from listening to others. Of course, we have the aspects we mentioned in the previous chapters of ego, false beliefs, willful ignorance, and resistance to objectivity. Sometimes, we're just in denial and only see what we want to see (more on this later). Sometimes, we don't know enough to know that we are wrong (more on this later too). A general lack of outside perspective or experience can also contribute—how open would someone raised to believe that electricity is magic be to any belief system that is not rooted in magic?

Someone else might confuse an anecdote as evidence and remain steadfast in their belief based on that.

Additionally, people seek comfort and security. They prefer confirmation rather than disruption. Being open-minded is uncomfortable and scary. At the very least, a natural inclination is to seek a path of least resistance, which allows them to save the most energy.

Then there are those whose closed-mindedness is just a part of establishing domination over others. They're talking to fight, and thus they never listen to gain a deeper comprehension of something—they only do so to figure out how they're going to argue back. They're rarely interested in asking anybody questions, and when they *are*, they're usually the loaded kind. They state their opinions as absolute truth, almost as bait to be challenged.

Finally, there are those that fear the slippery slope. This is when someone sees credible information that counteracts their beliefs and refuses to pursue it further because they're afraid of what they'll discover.

Consider the following dialogue, stripped clean of offending content and focusing on a slippery slope argument against open-mindedness. Bob is tied his belief to the occurrence of a certain event in a certain year, while archaeologists and scientists have suggested that the event they're talking about happened two years *earlier.*

Bob's response to this research was somewhat confusing: "Even if those scientists are correct, if I changed my belief about that date, then I would have to change *everything* I believe in. Because it would mean I was wrong about other events and other dates, and the result of all my calculations would be wrong, and my entire belief structure would be disproven. *So, I'm just not going to go down that road."*

Most of these instances of closed-mindedness can be overcome through patience, evidence, and gentle coaxing. Through a series of experiments involving circuits, light bulbs, and batteries, you might be able to convince the magic believer that electricity is not, in fact, a bunch of tiny fairies being forced into slavery. People are instinctually closed-minded but not impossible to reason with.

But sometimes, a particular over-attachment to beliefs and opinions is tough to overcome. This is a danger zone, and it develops because some beliefs are so important to us that they become part of our *identity*. Identity is even more important than ego; you'll recover your sense of pride being momentarily crushed, but a blow to your identity will make you question your self-worth.

The most obvious example is with religious beliefs—it would be accurate to say that people attach their identities to these various beliefs. It even becomes a way to describe ourselves—*I'm a Christian/Muslim*, and so on. But it even pops up in so-called rivalries between fanbases of different television shows or technology companies—*I'm an Apple fanboy,* or *I'm on Team Jacob!* Being told that Team Edward is the correct way to be is a blow to you as a human—your opinions, worldview, and life.

It's entirely fair to describe oneself that way. But there can come the point where one's self-identity can get *so* wrapped up in those descriptors that they dictate our emotions and crowd out rational thinking. It's a pretty good indicator that if you start describing yourself with a belief, you're not going to be so open about it. That can breed a belief in absolute truth, always accompanied by closed-mindedness.

Our becoming emotionally wedded to our opinions mutates them into indisputable facts. That's when they become dangerous. When our beliefs possess our feelings, and we cement them as truth, we start to exclude, judge or dismiss the beliefs of others. Undue feelings of superiority take hold. And in that condition, it's impossible for *actual* truths—even provable, scientific ones—to get in.

Is there anything wrong with this? Not really. There's nothing wrong with believing in something strongly, of having faith in your convictions. There's nothing wrong with identifying yourself with beliefs. It's even okay to use them as sources of emotional comfort. But for our purposes, it makes real understanding and clear thinking extraordinarily difficult.

Whatever the level of intensity, *everybody* is closed-minded about *something*. However small, this rigidity leads to a world closed off to reality. If you prefer Apple technology to Android technology, you create a bubble in which no dissent is allowed. It doesn't take that many bubbles for you to become completely trapped in ego, comfort, security, certainty, emotional attachment, or dogma. It's a risky way of living.

This chapter will address ways to actively keep an open mind ripe for clarity of thought. We'll address some of the mental traps and tendencies that keep us from doing so, and we'll look for ways to blast through those inhibitors and get to the heart of reality.

Battle Confirmation Bias

We have mentioned confirmation bias briefly throughout this book, but it's time to dive into it because it's really the first place we must visit on our way to open-mindedness. It's an important tendency that we must avoid and something that we engage in frequently without any awareness.

Confirmation bias is rampant when one only pursues and listens to information or evidence in favor of a certain belief that we wish to be true. Doing so causes one to disregard, rationalize, deny, or steer clear completely of evidence that disproves or challenges that belief. It's not necessarily driven by ego so much as it is a desire to be correct.

You think, "women are bad drivers." You see a bad driver on the road one day, and turn your head to see who it is. A woman! *See? I knew it.* Your belief is confirmed. The next day you see another bad driver, turn to look, and it's a man. You conveniently forget this ever happened. At the end of the week, you genuinely believe that you have gathered sufficient "evidence" to prove that women are bad drivers. After all, didn't every bad driver turn out to be a woman? You certainly remember it that way. You believe you are gathering evidence; in reality, you merely act to confirm a preconceived belief.

Confirmation bias is the ultimate stance of seeing what you want and using that perception to prove a pre-chosen conclusion. It's where you start with a conclusion in mind, and work backward to make it your reality despite evidence directly to the contrary.

The simplest example is when you have a particular stance you want to support—for example, that dogs are loyal. So, you type into Google "dogs are very loyal"—obviously this is going to generate results about the loyalty of dogs, whereas if you type in (1) "are dogs loyal?", (2) "dogs' loyalty," or (3) "dogs are not loyal", you would get a broader range of the literature on dogs and loyalty. This particular stance does not have any consequences, but confirmation bias can also turn life-threatening.

For instance, you may support the conclusion that you are a world-class skier despite having only skied once in your life. Despite evidence that you constantly fell even on that one occasion, you explain it all away as "beginner's bad luck" and insist that you are ready for a double black diamond course—a type of course that involves cliffs that one could easily slip off of into oblivion.

You see other people's warnings as jealous, and you even find anecdotes from famous skiers about how they were amazing after only one class, ignoring the warnings of everyone else. You find a group of first-time skiers who advanced quickly for inspiration. All your detractors "don't know who you truly are," and "underestimate your abilities." Unfortunately, you end up persisting in the belief of your abilities, and you ski right off a cliff and perish.

That's how confirmation bias can tilt your interpretation of the world by restricting the flow of information. If you want to believe an opinion, then you'll feverishly seek out sources that will buttress your belief—even if it's false. And you'll ignore (No, I didn't see that!), deny (No, I refuse to believe that!), or rationalize (No, it's different here! *I'm* different!) sources that counteract or disprove your feelings—even if they're true.

It tends to lock us up in an echo chamber, where we only listen to a small number of the same voices and a narrow range of opinions, all of them in support of our view. For all intents and purposes, this is your world and reality; this is the majority view that seems to be the truth. With so many people (people *around* you, anyway) saying the same thing, how could you go wrong?

Though death by skiing is a fascinating phenomenon, an everyday example can help illustrate this better as to how we do it in our lives.

Enter Sally.

She's gone on two dates with John. After she returned home from the second date, she sent John a picture of a wedding ring that she liked and asked for John's mother's phone number. John is rightfully horrified. But Sally felt that she was simply acting assertively because she had asked five of her closest friends, and they all told her to do this. She also searched online and found one source (meant as satire) that told her to do this, while ignoring all the other search results that told her not to be so clingy so quickly. An echo chamber was created around Sally, leading to a detachment from reality and the situation at hand. Good thing John and Sally met at the date venues, and Sally didn't have his address!

It's never easy (nor much fun) to be diagnosed with confirmation bias. But once you realize where it's stemming from, it should motivate you to seek a course of action to lessen its impact: *argue against yourself.*

If you're certain of your opinion, then you should be able to identify the arguments *against* your opinion. After all, you know exactly what you are ignoring, denying, or rationalizing. The typical sequence of events is your opinion, an opposing argument, and your confirmatory reaction. What then? Continue that discussion. Make an honest effort to create a back and forth to see the merits and weaknesses of both sides.

If you give 100% effort to your own opinion, you must give 100% effort to the opposing opinion. Engage with it and ask why it exists. Ask about the different perspective that created that opinion. Question the evidence you like as harshly as you'd question the evidence you dislike. Hearing the other side of an argument will give you a much better ability to understand a different position, the different worldview or reality, and the factors involved that you never considered. Even if you don't change your opinion, you've opened up a channel that wasn't there before.

For example, maybe you're talking to someone who is bitterly opposed to the construction of a new park in your neighborhood that you support. You think a park would substantially increase the livability and comfort of your neighborhood, but your opponent doesn't think it's a good use of money.

Instead of trashing the opposing view, ask why the view exists first. Maybe they feel the money's better spent on improving local roads; perhaps they'll tell a story of a relative who suffered severe injuries on a street that was in bad need of repair. Or maybe they feel that a park should only be built after other social services are fully funded and operational. Whatever their reasoning, try to get a story from them, and see if there's a solution you can work toward together.

You might find that you even start getting defensive with yourself in this process but attempt to engage in this from a perspective of curiosity, self-education, and seeking knowledge.

An important step is to write these arguments down to truly see for yourself what both sides are represented by. Try outlining your viewpoints, and then make up arguments *against* them. Provide the same amount of arguments for each, and directly address the corresponding ones. Flip your Google searches as we did with discovering the loyalty of dogs earlier. If evidence is presented, find it, and search for the opposite if it exists. Remember that evidence is objective, but reasoning and perspective is subjective—yours included!

After all this sweat and toil, you may find out that you don't believe your original argument as much as you thought you did. And that's the first step to cracking confirmation bias and starting to think openly. It's the simple realization that you should leave a 1% buffer of doubt and uncertainty for yourself, and being 100% certain about something takes work that you probably haven't performed—as you know from Bertrand Russell.

Our refusal to hear the opposing side isn't a sign of inner strength or resolve—it's the exact opposite. If we're so wound up with apprehension about giving an ear to somebody with different viewpoints, we're already powerless.

Follow the Evidence

As an extension of denying your confirmation bias, another aspect of openness and mental flexibility is to *follow the evidence*. Wherever it points is where you go. Inevitably, a narrative begins to unfold as you delve deeper and seek to understand. All you have to do is look in that direction without regard to how happy or unhappy it makes you.

You might find real evidence that supports your point of view—great. But you'll also find evidence that you don't necessarily want to face, the kind that offers cogent and reasonable arguments against your position. Even people who have devoted themselves to fearless truth-seeking might bristle at this evidence and try to avoid it. To a certain point, it's fine, but especially if it pierces the shields of their cherished identity—religious, political, social, allegiance to a fictional movie character—they may try to sidestep it and turn it away.

You know what I'm going to say: That's exactly the evidence you should need to follow and follow to its utmost. It's a deceptively simple task—if you can let go.

Treat all the evidence you receive by the same standards of reliability. All of it needs to pass the same sniff test. You must be circumspect of all evidence, which means tending toward high-*quality* information more than high *quantities* of information.

Imagine an arrow pointing in one direction after reviewing some information and perspectives. This is a green arrow to symbolize that it is correct. However, you will have to be able to pick it out from a multitude of red arrows, which seem helpful but aren't. Sometimes, it's more important to eliminate those red arrows, as you can never quite be sure that you are indeed following the *green* arrow.

Beware of black-and-white thinking. Black-and-white thinking is easy. That's why people practice it. But it's also dangerous. Starkly contrasted, right-or-wrong belief systems are the downfall of modern civilization. Unfortunately, they're not going away anytime soon, but to maintain a path of intellectual openness, you must learn to avoid black-and-white thinking—and keep it from inserting it into your own beliefs.

Black-and-white thinkers only see two options for anything: "You're with us or against us." "If it's not Mars, it's Venus." "If I don't follow that red arrow, it must be this red arrow." If the evidence doesn't point one way, it definitely points to the other. Maybe the middle ground doesn't exist because it's more important for them to be certain than right.

But that's an error of epic proportions. If someone doesn't like the color red, it doesn't mean they like blue. One discovery does not necessarily rule out another, and there isn't a causal link between very many things.

Only a few truths are absolute, and they're the ones provable by evidence. But all other truths—more accurately, beliefs—are more nuanced. There's more to consider and think about when deciding what's true and what's not.

In their natural state, most people are not sharply one way or the other. The truth is the same. Perhaps the tendency for black-and-white thinking is because of the following point.

It's okay to be uncertain—it's not okay to pretend you know what you don't. Saying "Maybe" is a perfectly fine conclusion, and an opinion isn't mandatory. Being unknowledgeable about current issues simply isn't an option. Saying "I don't know" is almost *shocking* to some people, because they've internalized that statement as a sign of failure or some shortcoming. *All* of the arrows you can currently see might be incorrect.

Many of us offer an uninformed opinion off the top of our heads to avoid that appearance. We think it's better to have *some* insight—even if it's completely off-base—about something we don't understand than to remain quiet or express doubt. And then, as we do, we stick to that stance for no good reason.

Sure, uncertainty is uncomfortable or at least can be. But it shouldn't be so disarming that we try to conquer it by finding something, anything, to believe. The fear of being uncertain is why people accept conspiracy theories or the rantings of a charismatic cult leader. They may be completely without merit, but they admire the *sureness* they provide. Even if the beliefs are absolute rubbish, they're better than having no beliefs at all.

Almost invariably, the information they're getting is ill-formed, unsound, slanted, and even flat-out false. But that doesn't matter, because they feel like they know something. It doesn't even matter to them that they're not right—because it's important to feel *certain*.

Your biggest stumbling block in this situation is emotional. It is the emotion of anxiety you feel from a lack of certainty. You need to understand and believe that there's nothing wrong with being uncertain, that ambiguity is not an affliction. Some might even say that being uncertain or ambiguous is *exciting*, because it opens up possibilities. In any event, being uncertain is far, far more preferable to believing in something false.

De-stigmatize the dreaded three words "I don't know." You won't lose points in the eyes of others. In fact, they might even appreciate that you're the rare breed who doesn't feel they have to have a ready set of opinions about something they don't know anything about. It's much, much better to be unsure than to be misguided.

Just remember this: Your search for truth is rooted in a desire to *understand*. You're seeking *knowledge*—you are not necessarily seeking *answers*. The key to getting through that uncertainty is to accept the chance to test or confirm our beliefs.

Thinking "must" or "should". This is one of the leading causes of biased and closed-minded thinking. Like other shortcomings we have discussed, this leads to you looking at a set of evidence with a conclusion already in mind, based on how you picture something should occur, and trying to mold the evidence to fit that. It is when you expect the world to be different than it is, and it is the opposite of what you should do.

Must and *should* thoughts are beliefs that you unknowingly treat as fact. If they don't materialize, even after you see clear arrows to proceed another way, you'll still be hesitant to follow the evidence. For example, you could carry the belief that dogs "should" be friendly—how might this "should" hurt you if you encounter a wild dog frothing at the mouth with rabies? *Shoulds* and *Musts* masquerade as evidence, and for that reason, they are a red arrow to be avoided.

Beware of the Dunning-Kruger Effect. This was coined by Cornell psychologists David Dunning and Justin Kruger in the late '90s. Simply put, some people aren't informed or knowledgeable enough to know what they don't know. Even worse, they're usually over-confident in their abilities because there is little nuance and only simple questions and answers to them. The more they fall prey to this effect, typically the more confident they are in themselves.

Dunning-Kruger occurs in just about any setting where people assume they know best. You might see it during a chess match, where a novice feels that chess is extremely simple—while missing all the behind-the-scenes planning and nuance. It's just not possible to follow the evidence if you have no idea what you're looking for (and you don't know that you don't know).

Dunning himself recently noted that the effect isn't necessarily fatal. Many people appear to have it simply because they don't know the standards for success or accomplishment, so they're essentially flying blind, but giving themselves credit for keeping afloat. Once people become *aware* they suffer from Dunning-Kruger and acknowledge it, they can always reverse its effect by learning and putting it into practice.

You can take a few steps that will ameliorate the Dunning-Kruger effect. A lot of it involves things we've already talked about: being humble and realistic about your current state of being, not being intellectually lazy, and not thinking that you're above anybody else in terms of intelligence or accomplishment. The world is usually not devoid of complexity, so if you feel there is little nuance, you are probably missing entire levels of analysis. To combat this, embracing self-challenge is key because it turns out that if something appears too simple to be true, you probably just don't know what to look for.

Labeling. This is when you, quite naturally, attach labels to people, places, things, and perspectives. The problem is that any label's purpose is to reduce to a single word and the abbreviation of information. These labels, usually not carefully chosen or given much thought, go on to form your beliefs. These are hazards with relatively accurate and descriptive labels—what about when you unwittingly use labels that are ambiguous, inconsistent, or inaccurate?

One big risk with labeling is that instead of describing the specific situations or perspectives in isolation, you create negative and absolute labels. In such instances, it's not about the situation in the moment; it's rather about making judgments about all future circumstances based on what you have just observed. It's similar to when we confuse feelings for facts.

Jumping to conclusions is a theme that underlies everything that happens when you don't follow the evidence. Sometimes there is no battling this, but the key is always to slow down. Try to honestly answer when you have been fooled and made incorrect judgments, and when you have failed to see the whole picture. Think about interpersonal communications and how many misunderstandings you have experienced in your life, despite your best intentions and deep friendships.

Battle Social Influence

If we can characterize confirmation bias and following the evidence as something internal that you must battle to stay clear and open-minded, then the social influence is something external that we must battle. In other words, we must resist the influence of others and draw our own conclusions rather than parroting those of others or being overly dependent on them.

None of us prefer to think of ourselves in this way—essentially a follower. We all like to imagine that we have *free will* and are actively making our decisions and determining out own thoughts instead of the other way around. If you're not a follower, that means you're a leader.

Leaders blaze the trail and set the path instead of the other way around. They are strong-minded and are driven by a set of morals and convictions. Above all else, they alone determine their thoughts. The truth, however, is a bit uglier. What we might define as free will daily is just us being influenced in subtle and subconscious manners by other people and the settings we find ourselves in.

Here's a simple example.

If you walk into your new job and you find everyone wearing magenta shirts, you are probably going to find a magenta shirt as soon as you can for the next day, even though there is no dress code, and no one has ever mentioned anything about magenta shirts. Something in your mind will tell you that you should be wearing a magenta shirt, even though there are no rules about it and the people you've asked haven't mentioned it either. You might even feel uncomfortable if you don't buy one within the week.

We are heavily influenced by the people around us and the contexts we find ourselves in, to such a degree that free will is more accurately categorized as just another decision that depends on what we see and feel from others. Two infamous, landmark studies show just how much we are swayed by others and left closed-minded.

The Asch Conformity Experiment is the first study that digs deep into the concept of dubious free will. This study was conducted by Solomon Asch of Swarthmore College in the 1950s and broadly demonstrated the compulsion to conform and "fit in" despite our best instincts and interests.

The study was relatively simple and asked participants to conduct a vision test. There was only one subject in each run of the study, and the rest of the people present were Asch's confederates. They would attempt to influence the true participant to conform and act against their free will.

The participant sat around a table with seven confederates and was asked two questions:

Which line was the longest in Exhibit 2?

Which line from Exhibit 2 matches the line from Exhibit 1?

Below is what the participants saw and made their judgment on. When participants were asked this question alone, through writing, or without confederates who would provide a range of answers, they consistently answered in the same way: Obviously, Line C and Line A, respectively.

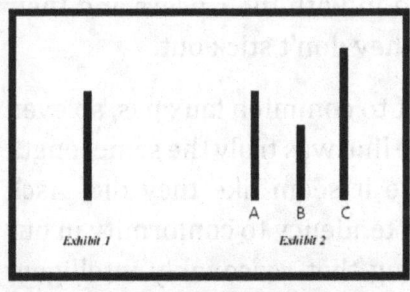

However, when confederates were present and provided incorrect answers, what followed was surprising.

When the true participant was surrounded by confederates who gave incorrect answers, such as stating that Line C was equal to Exhibit 1, or Line B was the longest in Exhibit 2, they also conformed their answers to be stunningly incorrect based on the social pressures of those around them. Over one-third of the true participants gave an obviously wrong answer, presumably because of the influence of peer pressure and the general feeling of, "What could I be missing that everyone else is seeing?" This feeling of confusion and wanting to avoid appearing stupid can cause someone to conform to something obviously wrong, which will make them appear stupid because they were trying to avoid that very thing. Asch successfully displayed that people, whether they believe it or not, wish to blend in with their peers and their environment, so they don't stick out.

People don't want to commit a faux pas, so even if they thought the line was truly the same length or not, they made it seem like they did. Asch commented, "The tendency to conformity in our society is so strong that reasonably intelligent and well-meaning young people are willing to call white black."

After the experiment, he had the opportunity to ask participants whether they actually believed their altered stances, and most did not and simply wanted to go along with the group because they did not want to be thought of as "peculiar." Others thought the group's judgment was correct and felt their new answer was correct as well.

These two approaches represent the two main reasons people appeared to conform and act against their free will. First, they wanted to be liked by the group and not seen as a "peculiar" outsider—a normative influence. They wanted to fit in and be seen as comparable to the group. Second, they conformed because they thought their information was faulty, and they wanted to use the group's judgment instead of their own. This is called an informational influence, where they doubted their own instincts and assumed others had more and better information than they did.

In either case, people's clarity of thought is subverted by emotional reactions (discomfort, anxiety) to what other people are doing. You can say that you chose to go along with other people's answers consciously, but in fact, it wasn't what you truly wanted to do.

This is how we end up wearing magenta shirts far more often than we think we should. You might start with buying only one, but by the end of a year, you'll probably have a closet full of magenta shirts just because it seems like the right thing to do to fit in. You want acceptance from the group not to appear "peculiar," and you feel there's a reason magenta is so prevalent, one you don't quite know yet.

We take cues on how to behave and think from other people, especially if it's an unfamiliar situation. For instance, if you show up at a fancy ball, you would look to how other people bow, stand, and interact so you can calibrate your own behavior. Where this takes a deviation into clarity of thought is where you go directly against what you know to be true just to conform. Asch's experiment was one instance where a correct answer was passed over, showing the true power of peer pressure and social influence.

Stanley Milgram's famous electrical shock experiment chronicled in his 1963 paper *Obedience to Authority: An Experimental View* is one of the most important and famous psychological experiments ever conducted. And for our purposes, it demonstrates how we are slaves to authority and generally don't act in a way we want when ordered to do something under the guise of duty. In more recent times, remembering the conclusions of Milgram's experiment can explain how atrocities as unthinkable as torture of prisoners of war have happened, or even how genocide was allowed to rise to prominence during World War II.

People aren't inherently evil and don't necessarily use their free will to inflict such harm. Instead, Milgram showed us another explanation for why people act in atrocious ways while remaining very human at heart. It can serve as a general lesson on why people capable or who have done dark things aren't different from you or me.

Milgram began his research at Yale University in the 1960s with the initial impetus of studying the psychology of genocide. He began to theorize that people weren't necessarily evil, twisted, or even different from those who *didn't* commit genocide, but that it was rather a reflection of authority, orders, and the perception of a lack of accountability. In other words, if you were just being told what to do and you were conditioned to follow orders without question, there was a pretty good chance you were going to be able to do anything.

After all, that is why soldiers go through boot camp and are berated endlessly by drill instructors—it is a process designed to promote obedience and conformity, even in the worst conditions that combat will present.

However, Milgram's experiment showed it wasn't only trained soldiers who could fall victim to such blind obedience and have their free will taken away from them. Milgram built a "shock machine" that looked like a device that would be used to dole out torture, but in reality, it did nothing and was mostly a series of lights and dials. This would be his tool for exposing human nature.

His experiment worked on the premise that the participant was administering a memory test to someone in another room, and if the unseen person made a mistake on the test, the participant was instructed by a man in a lab coat to punish them with electric shocks stemming from the "shock machine." The shocks would escalate in intensity based on how many wrong answers were given. Before starting the experiment, the participant was given a 45-volt electric shock that was attached to the shock machine. 45 volts was where the shocks would begin and then increase in 15-volt increments with each mistake. The shock machine ranged up to 450 volts, which also had a warning label reading "Danger: Severe Shock" next to them, and the final two switches were also labeled "XXX."

The unseen test-taker followed a script of getting the vast majority of the questions incorrect. As the participant administered shocks, goaded on and encouraged by the man in the white lab coat, the actor would cry out loudly and begin to express pain and anguish, begging them to stop and eventually falling completely silent.

Despite this, pushed on by the man in the white lab coat, a full 62% of participants administered the electrical shocks up to the highest level, which included the "XXX" and "Danger" levels. Milgram only allowed the man in the white lab coat to encourage with neutral and relatively benign statements such as "Please continue" and "It is essential that you continue."

In other words, the participants weren't coerced within an inch of their life to, in their perception, shock someone to unconsciousness or death! 62% reached the 450-volt limit, and none of the subjects stopped before reaching 300 volts. At 315 volts, the unseen actors went silent. The participants weren't being forced to do this; neither were they yelled at or threatened. How could these results have occurred?

Are people just callous, with little regard for human life and suffering outside of their own? That can't be true. What's more likely to be true is how persuasive the perception of authority can be in subverting our free will. We will act against our wishes if we sense that we are being ordered to by someone who has power over us, no matter how arbitrary.

This obedience to authority and sense of deference can even push us to electrocute an innocent person to implied death. Suddenly, things such as genocide, the Holocaust, and torturing prisoners of war don't seem so far-fetched. We like to think we have hard limits on what we could inflict on others, but the results of Milgram's experiments showed otherwise—our free will can be completely bypassed because of a simple display of authority.

Milgram noted other factors might be the feeling that because there was an authority figure, they would hold no accountability and be able to say, "Well, he told me to!" When the participants were reminded they held responsibility for their actions, almost none of them wanted to continue participating in the experiment. Many even refused to continue if the man in the white lab coat didn't take explicit responsibility. Additionally, it was an unseen victim they had never met before, so a degree of separation and dehumanization allowed actions to go further.

In the end, a normal person was shown to have followed orders given by another ordinary person in a white lab coat with a semblance of authority, which culminated in killing another person. It was quite the discovery in terms of what drives and motivates people. It was powerful evidence that clarity of thought is subject to all manners of delusion and influence.

These experiments prove the simple fact that who we think we are doesn't matter. We can have the clearest of thoughts, which also doesn't matter. What matters more in determining how we think and act are our surroundings, contacts, and the unique set of pressures that come with each context. Being open-minded means considering all sides, not deciding based solely on someone else's influence.

Let's tie this all back to autonomous, free and independent thought. If you hope to be a truly independent thinker, you will need to learn how to go against the grain. This may mean learning to recognize and push against your tendency towards confirmation bias, or it may mean deliberately going against public opinion, peer pressure and social influence. Some of the world's finest thinkers have encountered unthinkable levels of stubbornness, resistance and pushback from those who value ease and conformity about truth and clarity. Seek independent thought, and you may find yourself coming face to face with this pressure yourself!

Summary:

- An integral part of crystal-clear thinking is to be open-minded. Being open-minded means hearing evidence or an argument and not making an instant judgment. It means being able to say, "I don't know" and resist that feeling of uncertainty. These are all difficult because we are wired to do the opposite.

- The most glaring example of this is confirmation bias, wherein we are deaf and blind to evidence that doesn't support what we think. In other words, we see what we want to see, and we can make a belief appear out of thin air. This is dangerous because it brings the ability to ignore reality. You eventually become entrenched in an echo chamber of reinforcing information that will lead you astray.

- Confirmation bias is also the most prominent way that we fail to simply follow the evidence. If we perform research and keep an open mind, our task is simple: just follow the arrows where they point. But all too often, we are seduced into following the wrong arrows. These include the cognitive distortions of focusing on "must" and "should", black-and-white thinking, the Dunning-Kruger Effect, and labeling.

- The last way we must struggle to keep an open mind and clarity of thought is concerning our social influences. The people around us can determine what we think and do, no matter how hard we try. This was proved in the Asch Conformity Test and the Milgram Shock Experiment. It doesn't matter how open-minded you are; your environment can push you strongly in one way despite your best intentions.

Chapter 3: Freedom from Flawed Thinking

Somewhere along the line, it became fashionable for certain kinds of schools to claim that they didn't teach pupils *what* to think but rather *how* to think. This focus on quality rather than content is a keystone of independent, original thought, but is much rarer in real life than most would like to think.

Some are blessed with academic intelligence, otherwise known as pure book intelligence. We can memorize facts and data, process and manipulate information, and regurgitate it in the format most likely to win marks and points on standardized tests. Being good at school is a narrow and specialized skill set, but it has limited applicability in the real world – because it concerns the *what* and not the *how*. You probably know someone who earnt straight As in school or has a PhD but has some beliefs and real-world behaviors that are, quite frankly, stupid!

Practical intelligence is sorely lacking these days. It's also known as common sense, i.e., seeing the world for what it is. It's a style and quality of thinking rather than a particular set of thoughts. In reality, it turns out that *how* we navigate the world and approach, it is far more important than what we know about it.

Practical intelligence is about taking in your surroundings, ascertaining what's happening, and then making the best decision for you with the information you've got. This might seem to be the most important of thinking skills, but it's also never explicitly taught. We are mostly left to ourselves to figure it out, and this can easily explain a lot of the mental errors we observe people making daily–even those we ordinarily consider intelligent.

Going out of business sale? Okay, I need to buy everything right now.

This news article makes an outrageous claim without a citation? Well, that sounds about right, so I will now believe it with all my might.

If I feel something is true, then it must be true.

And so on. You may be able to spot these errors at the moment, but these thoughts occur automatically throughout our lives, and we certainly don't catch all of them. Who knows what significant life decisions you've made off the back of such unexamined thoughts! Let's take the first step into using our brains for good, instead of using them to fall into traps and follies. It's always about looking underneath the surface and stopping the assumption that you can trust what you see, hear, and feel.

We've all got that distant relative or long-lost friend who sends us occasional e-mails outlining the details of an off-the-rails conspiracy theory. This week, it's the outrageous, infuriating, and *"totally proven!"* theory that the government uses children's television shows to send secret messages to obey their orders. And unfortunately, you've opened this e-mail from your relative, even though you should know at this point that when something from this person is labeled "IMPORTANT!" it most certainly will not be.

"Look at this data from the National Alphabet Council!" they write. "It shows that Big Bird from *Sesame Street* triggers a part of your brain that responds positively to authority! It's all in his beak! Over 85 percent of all *Sesame Street* watchers report experiencing electrical seizures every time Big Bird appears onscreen! I learned all this from Jack Sprat's podcast *Under Attack!*

Stop your kids from watching *Sesame Street* unless you want them to be lackeys to an authoritarian dictator!"

Something strikes you as . . . *fishy* about this particular story.

The National Alphabet Council? What is *that*? And all those kids reporting seizures? Geez, you know some people with kids. You'd think you would have heard about this by now. And isn't Jack Sprat that guy who claimed pasteurized milk makes school kids pledge allegiance to Satan?

All right, so you Google "National Alphabet Council." To your utter lack of surprise, there's no such organization with its website. But you did find a link to a Snopes.com article that reveals the National Alphabet Council was used as a "source" to prove that *Green Eggs and Ham* was a Communist manifesto.

First off, this e-mail didn't pass the sniff test—something just seems *off* about it. Next, you don't find *any* data corroborating the reports on electrical seizures from kids watching *Sesame Street*. You see no evidence that Big Bird's beak is sending out coded messages to children. However, you do find something about Jack Sprat: an interview he gave with a major metropolitan newspaper in which he admits,

"Look, I'm just an entertainer. I make people feel a certain way. If I believed half the stuff I talk about, I wouldn't be doing a show. I'd be curled up in the corner of my room, waiting for the world to end. Instead, I get a handsome paycheck!"

You send this information to your relative. They respond back, "Well, that's interesting. I haven't thought about that. But that Jack Sprat is so *passionate* about his beliefs, and he's a great communicator. I think I'll stick to what he says. Say, have you heard the Illuminati is monitoring your online dating profiles?"

Humans all want certainty. We want to be sure of our beliefs—uncertainty is an uncomfortable feeling that we try to eliminate every time we make a decision or plan an event. And we want it fast—now, if not sooner.

Many of us consider doubt and hesitation as roadblocks to getting things done or signs of insecurity in our thoughts. Since we were young, we've even been taught that *speed* of certainty is a sign of intelligence and solid thinking. As a result, we often race to get our beliefs affirmed by the first source we find and adopt them as proven truth.

This path presents a critical error in our natural thinking instincts, and it's a tendency we must veer away from for better, smarter thinking. *Certainty is more important than accuracy.* We tend to seek out confirmation that's more passionate than truthful. We're more impressed by someone on television mounting a fervent argument about an issue, instead of a calm, reasoning, boring person who simply lays out the facts as they are. If someone's acting intensely about their beliefs, we're inclined to think they must have the truth on their side, and we get swept up right along with them.

Practical intelligence is about seeking truth, not prioritizing removing *uncertainty* over establishing certainty. They aren't the same thing. Eliminating uncertainty means giving serious thought to what's causing doubt—in our opening short story, that would be looking up the National Alphabet Council to find out if they're on the up-and-up. Establishing certainty is simply glomming on to the first "fact" that soothes the uncomfortable feeling of uncertainty, insecurity, and simply *not being sure of something*.

This first chapter is about not accepting anything at face value because face value tends to deceive intentionally. It's about seeking the truth and nothing but the truth. You can imagine this might make you a pain in the butt to deal with, but it's not about that. It's about the fact that every situation has at least some complexity and nuance underneath it. And if you keep digging, frequently, things are completely different from what they seemed at first glance.

Making this whole process harder is the fact that the brain loves certainty so much that it processes it as a *reward*. The brain perceives uncertainty as a threat that needs to be extinguished. The sooner we can remove that threat with certainty, the better, no matter how shaky the certainty's foundation.

The most effective thinking models help us quickly decipher and comprehend what's happening in our world. They make it easier to decode and interpret what we see and lead us to consider matters more thoroughly. Ultimately that course will be more rewarding than slap-dash validations of what we *prefer* to believe.

One helpful thought structure could be called "*strong opinions loosely held*." This means being positive and assured about what you believe, but open-minded enough to hear out viewpoints that might challenge your own. It also means accepting that there's nothing weak or embarrassing about changing your mind. Doing so with a solid grip on the facts is a sign of your mental *strength*; merely agreeing with the crowd is the *real* weakness.

Of course, this is easier said than done. After all, our brains are hungry for assurance and anxious in the face of disbelief. But we can train our brains to go more deeply beyond appearances and uncover the hidden details we don't see at first glance.

Curious as a Cat

The most powerful tool we have in overcoming our desire for certainty and looking beneath the surface isn't pre-existing intelligence or judgment. It's simple curiosity. However, many of us have not been truly, genuinely curious since we were little children. Why? Because somewhere along the line, we decided that the feeling of certainty was preferable to uncertainty. Because we have gotten into the habit of rushing towards a known, graspable conclusion (no matter the quality or value of that conclusion) in favor of staying in an open-ended, undecided state for as long as possible. Basically, it's because our ego got in the way.

From discovering fire and the wheel to the theory of relativity, all human knowledge sprang from someone being curious. It came from a drive to know more about the nature of the world. Nobody made these grand leaps from a position of thinking they *already knew*. They got there because they had the simplicity and humbleness to say, *Wow, this is weird. I have no idea what's going on here. I wonder what this is? I wonder what happens when I...?*

A question is infinitely more valuable than a statement regarding independent thought. Ask a question, and the world responds. Make a claim, and your dialogue with reality stops.

Curiosity drives one to dive deeply into the nuts and bolts until they come to a solid comprehension of a subject or situation. And when they get to that point, they're eager to learn *more*. It's a self-perpetuating trait; the more you have of it, the more you want it. And if you have enough of this one mindset, you will be well-positioned for deeper thinking.

Curiosity is a direct path to practical intelligence. Pursuing your curiosity will help you learn and perceive things that other people won't. Developing your inquisitiveness is vital to building your knowledge and awareness. Every field of thought or knowledge, without a single exception, is easier to learn if you keep your curiosity front and forward. It's how you can naturally get to the heart of things and comprehend deeply.

But curiosity isn't automatic, and it's not something you just will into existence.

Furthermore, some of us are blocked from curiosity because of fear: we tend to have severe anxiety about the unknown, and that anxiety can be particularly high when we're about to *find out* about the unknown.

We need to delve more deeply into the nature of curiosity to understand how it works and how we can use it. It's a far more versatile tool than you might initially expect, and can help you think in smarter ways. Think of this as a preliminary mindset to digging beneath the surface effectively on any topic.

Most of us would think, understandably so, that being curious is just a simple matter of having a higher interest in learning things or having new experiences. When we say someone is "naturally curious," we usually mean they are more motivated by this interest than other people. But in reality, there's a lot more to curiosity than simply having a strong desire to know more—people can become curious for quite a few distinctly different reasons.

Psychology professor Todd B. Kashdan from George Mason University spent a considerable amount of time researching the nature of human curiosity. Kashdan sought to nail down the diverse characteristics of curiosity into what he called "dimensions."

Kashdan conducted a study with over four hundred participants who answered three hundred personality questions. Analyzing the data he received, Kashdan developed a model of curiosity that identified *five* dimensions of curiosity. These aspects reveal how certain people are motivated to be curious in the first place. Knowing these dimensions and how they work might help you fire up your own curiosity engines. Kashdan's dimensions include:

1. Joyous exploration. When considering the nature of curiosity, this dimension is probably what we're picturing: the simple thrill of discovering and experiencing things we don't yet know about. The joyous explorer views new knowledge as a component of personal growth, which is its own reward for them. They're genuinely *excited* about reading all of Shakespeare's plays, trying sushi for the first time, or riding cross-country in a race car. Amassing a wealth of different experiences and knowledge simply makes them happy.

2. Deprivation sensitivity. On the other hand, this branch of curiosity is more about anxiety. Someone working from this dimension feels apprehensive or nervous about their lack of information—being "deprived" of knowledge makes them uneasy. To reduce this pressure, they engage their curiosity. The deprivation sensitivity dimension comes into play when we're trying to solve a problem, getting up to speed with our comprehension, or considering complicated ideas.

For example, if you're balancing your bank accounts and find you've spent more than you have on record, you get a little nervous, which in turn makes you go through your receipts to see if you've missed anything. If you're taking a philosophy class and the material's going way over your head, you feel anxious about your abilities and study a little harder (if you haven't let fear stop you, that is). When you finally discover the information you're seeking, your discomfort will—theoretically—stop.

3. Stress tolerance. Whereas deprivation sensitivity relates to how uncomfortable one feels about *not* having certain knowledge, the stress tolerance dimension focuses on the uneasy feelings of *getting* that knowledge or taking on a new experience. People with high stress tolerance in their pursuits are more likely to follow their curiosity. On the other hand, someone who can't deal with the uncertainty, disorder, or doubt that arises when exploring new ideas or having new experiences is less likely to let curiosity lead them.

Take two people who have never been on a roller coaster before and are in line to do so at an amusement park. Both of them are at least a little nervous about it because it's a new thing for them. One of them is more willing to confront their fears—they've done so before with other things and have always survived—so they're able to fight through their anxieties and get onboard. However, the other one lets their fear reduce them into a quivering mass of exposed nerves. They have to take the chicken exit and miss out on the roller coaster.

The first person clearly has a higher ability to tolerate stress, go past their fears, and follow their curiosity for a new experience. As for the second person, well, let's hope they *really* like the merry-go-round because that's pretty much all they can handle.

4. Social curiosity. This dimension of curiosity is simply the desire to know what's going on with other people: what they're thinking, doing, and saying. We indulge this curiosity by interacting with or watching others. We'll have a conversation with a friend because we're interested in a movie they just saw, or we want to hear their opinions on current events, or we just have to share in the latest gossip they've heard.

Social curiosity can also come from a more detached point of observation. A great example of this is people-watching in a crowded place, like a bus stop or Central Park. We might see a couple having a spat, or a couple of kids playing a game they just made up, or a man walking his pet duck. (It happens.) Based on what they're doing or saying, we might form certain judgments or opinions about how they are or behave in a more private situation. Curiosity drives us to study them.

5. *Thrill-seeking.* This aspect is similar to the stress tolerance dimension, except a thrill-seeker doesn't just tolerate risk — they actually *like* it. A thrill-seeker is more than happy to place themselves in harm's way just so they can gain more experience. For them, it's worth the gamble of physical jeopardy, social disavowal, or financial ruin just to have an adventure or encounter something new.

Look no further than Richard Branson, the hugely successful entrepreneur, for a thrill-seeking example. He's tried to balloon around the world. He's tried to race a boat across the Atlantic. He's stood valiantly in the path of oncoming storms that destroyed everything else in the immediate vicinity. Branson claims to have had *seventy-six* "near-death experiences," including one where he went over the handlebars of the bicycle he was riding. Branson escaped with only minor injuries as he watched his bike go off the edge of a cliff. Clearly, Branson feels extremely comfortable in situations where there's an element of danger. That's your thrill-seeker.

Curiosity is pretty easy and automatically generated for the joyous explorer and thrill-seeker. It's the same for the socially curious, depending on the situation and who surrounds them. For these three dimensions, curiosity is a welcome and comfortable condition. If you're aware of the positive benefits of something, it's easier to indulge in them. But we may not always feel that way, so we can't depend on it.

If you're resistant to curiosity, you might serve yourself by considering the origins of your anxiety. If you're feeling awkward about not being "in the know" or left out of the loop, you could use that motivation to drive you to amend that situation (deprivation sensitivity). If you're unable to fight through your fears, consider ways to rationalize them and get stronger (stress tolerance). Overall, we just want to understand what drives us toward and, conversely, what prevents us from embodying a curious mindset. Knowing the driving motivation helps.

The remainder of this chapter will look at techniques and approaches that can at least *simulate* a sense of curiosity to help bring you to new knowledge and experience—therefore helping you go beyond the surface level and get to the bottom of things.

We can't all naturally think, "Hey, what does that *really* mean?" so these mental models will help you reach that point methodically.

A Skeptic's View
Let's look at another crucial quality that all independent thinkers possess: doubt.

Skepticism is a model for understanding what you're looking at and gaining a truthful view of it. The word "skepticism" is frequently misunderstood, sometimes labeled an undesirable trait. The thesaurus will tell you that this word is synonymous with *mistrust*, *suspicion* or *pessimism* – but ask any philosopher, and they will tell you that nothing could be further from the truth!

When someone says they're skeptical about a certain thing, they might ruffle the feathers of somebody else who thinks they're just letting their negativity get in the way. Why'd they have to ruin all the fun with their skepticism?

Some people use the word "skeptical" interchangeably with the word "cynical"—but there's a world of difference between the two. Except for both trains of thought involving a measure of disbelief, they couldn't be more different.

The skeptics belonged to an ancient Greek school of philosophy, although the general principles were practiced worldwide throughout history. The classical skeptics actively questioned the possibility of knowledge or argued that judgment should be completely suspended if there is insufficient evidence to warrant belief. While it might get pretty tiresome to believe that truth is not ultimately knowable except in probabilistic terms, modern skeptics make a good argument for not taking anything for granted, knowledge-wise.

A skeptic approaches everything from the standpoint of reason and learning; they're open-minded but picky about requiring evidence. They don't believe something unless they have a reason to.

However, this is different from broadly mistrusting any viewpoint you don't already agree with, or just any viewpoint in general. Sometimes, people may claim to be skeptics but are merely describing a stubborn closed-mindedness – they're firm and fixed in their beliefs. They believe everything in life will progress in a certain way, and there's no point in questioning it. Even hard, verifiable evidence may not sway their beliefs. For example, we all know that the media can lie and that falsehoods can and do appear in the news. But consider these three different attitudes:

1. "You still read the paper? Pshh, I don't see the point. It's *all* lies and propaganda. You can't trust a single word…"
2. "I read the BBC because they're trustworthy and neutral. They're the gold standard. They wouldn't lie."
3. "You shouldn't believe everything you read. Could this news article be fair and balanced? Maybe. Maybe not. I haven't got enough evidence yet to decide either way."

Can you see the difference? Blandly announcing that nothing can be known or trusted is mere nihilism. This is rebelling for the sake of rebelling, and has nothing to do with independent thought. Making fixed, sweeping claims about the nature of things (whether these sweeping claims are flattering or not-so-flattering) speaks to a closed-mindedness that is the opposite of real skepticism. The third attitude is the skeptical one –merely the dignity of not making any claims, or believing anyone else's claims until there is sufficient evidence to do so. This, naturally, ties into the ability to tolerate uncertainty and to temper the ego enough to keep saying, "I don't know."

Cynicism is dangerous because it implies no answers to anything in life. A cynic believes that matters have already been determined, and there's no point in challenging them. Cynicism shuts down investigation and discourages interest. That's dangerous because it leads to hopelessness. Skepticism, on the other hand, has a positive goal of discovering real truth (incidentally, the ancient Greek school of the Cynics practiced a style of philosophy very aligned with the themes of independent thought explored in this book, and completely disconnected from the modern usage of the term "cynical").

A skeptic seeks to find irrefutable truth, or as close as they can get to it. This, by definition, involves going beneath the surface and determining what's really in front of you. The word itself derives from the Greek *skeptikos*, which translates to "inquiring" or "looking around." A skeptic's mission is to question. A skeptic's mind is trained to look for the basic facts, impartial to any bias or agenda. This is probably an unnatural way for most of us to be thinking, but it can shed light on how much you leave uncovered.

Skeptics don't settle for having blind faith or wishing truth into existence. They don't *want* to burst anyone's bubble, but neither do they want to fill someone up with false confidence. They just want to understand, and they do not discriminate between the conclusions that might surface. They are the impartial judge of a criminal court, with similar standards and adherence to intellectual honesty. They see things in only black and white, as you also must. There can be no wiggle room.

Skeptics operate only on *evidence*. They must have proof that the assertions of other people work or are completely true. They can't accept facts simply at face value. Before a skeptic can decide something's real, they need to see confirmation in the form of data or consistently repeated results. The mere fact that someone just "heard somebody say something" is nowhere close to being evidence. That's merely an anecdote, and the plural of anecdotes is *also* not evidence.

A healthy skeptic always considers and questions the source of certain information—and no matter how high up or acclaimed that source may be, they're still subject to being confirmed by evidence. A source may have impeccable credentials, a gleaming reputation, and considerable fame or authority. All of that's great. *They still need to have evidence.*

Skepticism will feel more satisfying the more you use it, and you'll be less prone to flawed thinking, counterfeit facts, and weak arguments. Just make sure you don't become an annoying pedant with this newfound power of scrutiny you've found. Skepticism is a mindset of withholding judgment until you are sure the truth is plain to see.

This pursuit of truth and reality might echo something you're already familiar with, the *scientific method*. Indeed, skeptics resemble scientists more than anything else for their strict standards of proof. The scientific method is a time-proven process for gathering information scientists have used for centuries to test their theories. It works by scrutinizing observations and assumptions to ensure that the truth is discovered. For instance, if someone observes that it becomes colder at night, there would be no way of proving this truth unless data was collected during daytime and nighttime and compared.

The scientific method is generally considered to consist of five stages: asking a question, constructing a hypothesis, testing by experimentation, analysis of results, and forming a conclusion. In fact, this process exactly mirrors skepticism. An assertion without evidence or fact is essentially an opinion, and certainly nothing close to the truth.

Thus, to put everyday statements to the test, you're going to have to conduct an experiment, collect data, and analyze results empirically. Skepticism leads you down a line of inquiry and discovery that cuts out the assumptions and opens doors of truth.

Now that we've established that "skepticism" isn't a dirty word and is a hallmark of thinking smarter, how does one actually use it to evaluate the relative truthfulness of a claim? Here's a skeletal guideline for approaching a topic with appropriate skepticism.

1. Intake the statement. Fully absorb the meaning and implications of the claim after it's been made. Even if it sounds ridiculous to you at first hearing, at least pretend that it's a serious and meaningful belief. Give your source the benefit of the doubt for this one brief step. This will allow you to give it the attention it deserves, if even just to poke holes in it. When we dismiss, we don't pay attention.

2. Question the source. Consider the viability of the source of information. Then, consider the possible intentions of such a source. If it's a publication, media outlet, or website, gauge its reputation and agenda—there are plenty of legitimate-looking sources that aren't above distorting or stretching the truth to serve an agenda. If it's a friend, relative, or acquaintance, ask them to tell you where *they* got the information (without devolving into an intense argument, if possible).

3. Search for supporting arguments or information. If a certain claim has "gone public," there's probably ample information supporting it that you can easily find on the web. Find the arguments in favor of the statement you're researching—and again, question the sources as you go.

4. Search for opposing arguments or information. Repeat Step 3, but this time, look for statements or sources that either deny or criticize the information you're looking up. Be aware of the possibility of confirmation bias on your part while doing this step—don't discount opposing views or gravitate toward unreliable sources because they'll back up your own beliefs. Give yourself a higher standard of truth.

5. Question your findings logically. Here's where you put together what you've learned and weigh the likelihood of the statement being true or false. I like to write things down as a way of thinking through them, and you can do that by listing pros and cons, making a mind map, or drafting a persuasive essay for yourself. Or you can simply do some heavy contemplation in your head without writing anything down. Remember, you seek evidence, not certainty, and you don't need an explicit answer. You just want to look beneath the surface. Wherever the evidence points is where you look.

If you find the original claim viable, then you agree. If you've found too much doubt or contradictory evidence, you disagree. If you've seen compelling evidence for *both* sides and can't reconcile it right now, you can decide to leave it for the time being. Again, what's important is truth, not certainty.

The Critical Thinker

Critical thinking is the act of delaying gratification instead of accuracy and a three-dimensional understanding of the nuances presented to you. It's not popular as a way of navigating life, but it's how you will learn to look beneath the surface of any statement.

The goal of critical thinking isn't to produce a quick, easily digestible answer. In fact, it's not even to provide any certifiable conclusion whatsoever. Instead, critical thinking is to make a topic more transparent. The essence of critical thinking centers not on answering questions but on questioning answers. The approach is different, but the end goal is the same as skepticism's—to find the truth of the matter.

Rather than provide a rock-solid, inarguable conviction, critical thinking expands your viewpoint and gives you several ways to look at a situation or problem. It gets you past the external noise and easy answers to show you the whole scope of a circumstance or issue. It allows you to discuss information or a topic, even if only with yourself. That's where you'll learn more than what meets the eye.

The questions you use in critical thinking go beyond standard "just the facts, ma'am" inquiries. Instead, they challenge the answerer to probe the reasons for a subject's importance, its origins, relevance, and countering or alternative beliefs. They can be applied to any subject—even with some adaptation, scientific or mathematical principles. The goal isn't to get you to agree or disagree with a given doctrine but just to understand the totality of its meaning.

Let's try an example: *the theory of gravity*. All you need to know is that it is generally one of the laws of physics that govern our planet and the universe as we know it. We might think we know what it is, but subjecting it to a line of critical thinking questions would probably uncover the fact that it's not what you first thought.

Here are some questions you could use to critically evaluate the topic. I'm not going to attempt to answer them because I wasn't a physicist, at least last time I checked. But I did look up enough to form some decent questions, and the main point of this exercise is to show how they can be phrased:

What makes the theory of gravity important? This question seeks out why the theory of gravity deserves to be discussed.

Which details of the theory of gravity are important and why? This question gets down into the specific elements of the theory of gravity and how they affect certain factors of a body's motion.

What differentiates the theory of gravity from other theories? Why? This question seeks to discover why the idea does or does not have special significance.

What is an example of the theory of gravity? This question seeks to gain understanding through a concrete example.

What are the differences between the theory of gravity and other physics laws? This query compares two different models and allows you to understand what sets one model apart from the other.

How is the theory of gravity related to quantum physics? This question sets up a description of how the subject relates to other existing knowledge.

What evidence can you provide for or against the theory of gravity? This question forces acknowledgment of both positive and negative aspects of the subject. Each subject or topic has weaknesses and strengths regarding its applicability and universality.

What patterns do you notice in the theory of gravity? This helps you search out repetitive elements and cause-and-effect relationships, almost always indicating importance.

What are the advantages and disadvantages of the theory of gravity? This question sets up another comparison between the possible effects of the theory of gravity.

When might the theory of gravity be most useful, and why? This question looks for an example of how the concept is used in the real world and can affect your life.

What criteria would you use to assess whether the theory of gravity is accurate? This question seeks how to establish hard proof that a concept is working or not and introduces the concept of specific metrics.

What information would you need to make a decision about the theory of gravity? This question addresses how Keynesian models can thrive and what contextual information is important.

Do you agree that the theory of gravity works? Why or why not? This question encourages you to use your reasoning to judge the merit of a certain concept.

How could you create or design a new model of the theory of gravity? Explain your thinking. This question urges you to reimagine the concept following your own ideas and project how they could work in the future.

Whew. That's many questions. It's only a fraction of the many sides and angles from which you can examine any given issue. None of them are answered in definitive terms, nor can they be. But their open-ended nature encourages you to pursue the facts from an objective standpoint. Is this beginning to sound circular and repetitive? It can indeed be a never-ending and tedious exercise, but it becomes more meaningful if you keep the purpose of discovery and perspective at the forefront.

At this point, you may have used all your answers to formulate a theory or conclusion—or perhaps you've come across conclusions from others that address *their* interpretation of what the facts mean. But as with the questions you've just asked, the ideas you come across (even your own) should *also* be subjected to the same inquisition as to whether the conclusions are sound and hold up.

The first few questions should address the structure of the conclusion, whether it comes from a sound basis in reasoning. A second set of questions focuses on the quality of the conclusions and supporting arguments. We can see this through the same example of our theory of gravity model:

What are the issues and conclusions of the theory of gravity? This question addresses the foundation of the theory—the problem it was trying to solve—and the answers.

What are the reasons for your conclusions? A well-worded conclusion will list out the facts being used to support it. This question identifies what those facts are. And it's crucial to separate facts from anecdotes or *feelings*.

What assumptions are you using in your theory? If any variable factors are being used when the conclusion is formed, it's important to ferret them out. For instance, generally, the theory of gravity assumes that the laws of relativity apply, and a quantum singularity is nowhere nearby.

The next two questions seek to expose the shortcomings of thought that may have compromised the finding of the conclusions:

Are there fallacies in the reasoning? This question seeks out any inaccuracies, mistakes, or outright falsehoods in any of the reasons given.

How good is the evidence? This is how you check that the supporting facts behind the conclusion are airtight, from legitimate sources, and not discolored by bias or misinformation.

There's a chance that these questions might raise even *more* questions instead of answering all your inquiries. But again, that's the main point of this line of interrogation: to create a three-dimensional view of the topic you're investigating and not just stop at the first answer that looks "certain." Just because something is certain, it does not mean it is truthful.

But wait—critical thinking can go even more deeply, and we look to the Paul-Elder model for that. This approach is really going deeper into the rabbit hole, so to speak.

Paul-Elder Thinking

As might be apparent by now, improving the quality of your thinking, mental agility, and intelligence is never something that happens by accident, but rather something that you develop consciously and deliberately. Paul-Elder's framework for critical thinking is an extremely useful tool for training yourself intellectually and improving the *quality* of your thinking. This goes far beyond the set of questions we examined previously, shedding light on an entirely different mode of thought.

Thinking, as a function, can take on many characteristics. Just as physical movement can be graceful and in good form, thinking can be ordered and "correct" in an equivalent way—or clumsy and inelegant! By having intellectual standards, we establish a goal for the quality of thought we strive to achieve, and a big part of this is developing the skill and habit of critical thinking.

There are three main components to this framework:

The elements of thought or reasoning

The intellectual standards that should be applied to the elements of reasoning and

The intellectual traits of a critical thinker.

Let's begin with the first component. What are the elements of reasoning? Paul-Elder invites us to consider the units of the thought process itself, and assess them and their function. The authors proposed eight structural elements of reasoning:

Purpose

Questions

Point of view

Information

Inferences

Concepts

Implications

Assumptions

The first, *purpose*, is otherwise called your goal, objective or intention. A good critical thinker will be clear on their purpose. In other words, what are you trying to do here, and why? Does your goal need refinement, or expansion?

Another element is *the question itself*, the problem at hand, or the explored issue. Heisenberg famously claimed, "What we observe is not nature itself, but nature exposed to our method of questioning." Essentially, the quality of your inquiry matters, and will shape the rest of your critical thinking. To assess this element, ask yourself exactly what question you're trying to answer—and how you're stating that question. Could you frame it differently? What question is it, and could it be simplified? What form will the answer take? Is it a collection of several smaller questions?

Critical thinking also entails *gathering information*. If you've refined your question properly, you can gather relevant data and ignore data that isn't. Ask yourself whether the data you're gathering is not just relevant but also sufficient—i.e., is there enough of it? Is it accurate, and where did it come from? Is there some information you're missing? When you judge a piece of data as relevant, how exactly are you making that appraisal?

This will seamlessly lead you to another component, *inference*. You take in the data in front of you and draw conclusions from it. You interpret a set of facts to make a conclusive statement about it. However, to check that you're doing this correctly, you need to make sure your inferences actually flow logically from the evidence at hand. Does your interpretation make sense, or have you overlooked another possible angle? How did you reach your conclusion, and is it sound—i.e., did you make any unfounded assumptions? Inferences should be no more and no less than the data suggests. Here's the moment when you weigh up alternatives and question your assumptions.

From this flows another component, *concepts*. These are the theories, ideas, models, principles and laws we construct for ourselves to better help us understand the data we see. Again, concepts should be "justifiable," which means they should be appropriate to the data, not above or beyond it. Think carefully about your hypothesis, your claims and your assumptions. Try to find the core thread or principle and ask whether it's sufficiently clear, simple and relevant. Models are only good so long as they accurately reflect reality and allow us to make predictions. Does your model/theory do this? Why or why not?

Assumptions are another component we've already mentioned. We take these ideas for granted—consciously or unconsciously—even though there may not strictly be evidence for them. Ask what "obvious" pieces of information you're relying on or haven't properly looked at. What is being taken as a given, and what have you glanced over as unimportant? Is it? Look closely at all the steps you took to reach your conclusions or theories and ask if they're strictly supported by fact.

Implications and consequences are other components. If you settle on an idea or "truth," then some other ideas or truths will naturally and logically follow from the first. Actions have consequences, and thoughts have implications. Have you considered all of yours? What naturally follows if you do/claim something? What are the likely implications of taking your position or making your particular claim?

Finally, the eighth component is *point of view*, which is essentially your own unique perspective or orientation. Nobody has the privilege of a completely neutral frame of reference, so it's worth considering what your position is, and how it affects your reasoning. What are you focusing on and why? Is there another alternative perspective worth considering? Is your view reasonable—or does it ignore or amplify certain things? Consider how your point of view interacts with your assumptions and conclusions about what's in front of you. Does it contrast with others'? Are you giving yourself sufficient opportunity to challenge your orientation, or reconsider points of view that may be limiting you or causing you confusion or distress?

As you can see, each of these components makes up the complex and ever-changing process of our thinking. But without conscious awareness of *how* these components are working and interacting, the quality of our thought is unlikely to be high. You may run wild with unfounded assumptions, draw faulty conclusions or start extrapolating from incomplete data to prove a poorly conceived theory that is only backed up by partial, low-quality data. And you might not be aware that you are doing it!

Now, the whole reason for understanding these elements (the first part of the framework) is to appraise and improve upon them using your intellectual standards (the second part). In asking some of the questions we have above, we've seen how it's possible to challenge and explore each of these components. Paul-Elder had a more formalized way of doing this, which they called their "universal intellectual standards." These determine the *quality* of the reasoning, acting as a guide for thinking. You may perform some of these questions or appraisals deliberately at first, but the goal is to make them more habitual and automatic with time.

There are nine standards in total, and they can each, in turn, be applied to the elements listed above:

Clarity

Accuracy

Precision

Relevance

Depth

Breadth

Logic

Significance

Fairness

The first standard is *clarity*. To clarify is to cut down on confusion or vagueness, for instance, if you can elaborate on a claim, provide an example, or if you can paraphrase or simplify what you're saying. What seems like a great idea is often just a noisy, busy one that falls apart once you try to streamline it.

Accuracy is the standard of veracity. In other words, is it true? How could you tell? When checking a claim or a piece of information's truth, we also have to consider the source and motivation of the evidence itself. Ask why you have reason to believe this idea is true—or not. Is it better understood as a theory or opinion?

The standard of *precision* is also important. It's about specificity. Good thinking is about exact statements that are clear and focused. Are you being too general? Sometimes, good critical thinking means getting into the details of things to find *exactly* what you're saying.

Relevance is a standard already mentioned. This is not a value judgment, or a personal opinion, but rather an assessment of whether your thought has anything to do with your stated aim. It's necessary to bear the original question in mind, and keep comparing your questions, data and interpretations against it. Is what you're thinking about actually helping the issue at hand?

Depth is the standard that concerns levels of complexity. Are you thinking in too shallow a fashion? Have you carefully considered the difficulties and complexities of the issue at hand? This standard allows you to fully comprehend the scope of the question and the extent to which you're trying to solve it.

Similarly, *breadth* is a question not of the complexities and difficulties of an issue, but rather its natural boundaries. Have you considered enough alternative perspectives? Could the way you're thinking be expanded to include more? Here's where you weigh alternative points of view and expand the edges of your own.

Logic is an obvious standard that is harder to apply than it seems. It can be difficult to pick apart, but ask yourself whether what you're thinking strictly *makes sense*. If your thinking was an argument, would each premise flow naturally from the previous one? Does your claim follow from the evidence at hand? Are you solving the problem in the right terms? This standard is about making sure that the elements of your thinking are coherent.

The standard of *significance* is, in a way, about focus. Look carefully at the information you are choosing to focus on, and ask whether it is the most significant aspect of the issue at hand. Try to find the central issue of the matter and pay it proportional attention. Are you getting sidetracked by relatively insignificant details?

Look closely to sift through and filter out only what is most important.

Finally, the standard of *fairness* is significant, although a little tricky to handle. Here, you ask yourself whether your thinking is "justifiable." A good critical thinker considers the thinking of others and the purpose they're working toward. This standard is the closest to a moral aspect—are you using your intellect clearly and honorably, or are you merely attempting to win an argument or manipulate data to get what you want from the situation? This standard asks that we be reasonable and mature in the way we think and carefully consider the consequences.

Sadly, many people mistake intellectual rigor for a blood sport or think that developing critical thinking is a fancy way to assert intellectual dominance over others and win arguments. This is why it's crucial to consistently question your own position, your own intentions and your own limitations. A critical thinker is not someone really good at being right or showing their intellectual prowess. Rather, a critical thinker is someone who has trained themselves to be comfortable with being wrong, and who can use their cognitive processes not just to confirm what they already know, or wish was the case, but rather to enlighten themselves and reveal new avenues of thinking that might otherwise be hidden by sloppy or unexamined thought.

This leads us to the third and final part of the framework, which is the intellectual traits that Elder saw as belonging to those who have mastered critical thinking. In successfully applying our intellectual standards to the elements of reasoning, we fine-tune our mental apparatus and become better thinkers, period. Those who have developed the habit (and it's a *habit*, not a static personality trait) of critical thinking display specific characteristics, and in turn, can do well to cultivate the characteristics themselves.

These traits include:

Intellectual humility

Intellectual courage

Fair-mindedness.

Intellectual empathy (i.e., the ability to not just pay lip service to other points of view, but to actually deeply consider them as alternatives to their own view)

Confidence in one's own reasoning

Intellectual autonomy, i.e., the ability to "think for oneself"

Intellectual perseverance, i.e., the ability to push on with a confusing, unpopular or difficult concept.

Integrity

Though it's helpful to bear these qualities in mind when developing your mental capacity, they are better understood as emergent qualities that come from the consistent application of intellectual standards to the elements of your reasoning. In other words, we can idealize the strong, toned physiques of professional athletes, but we can only achieve that for ourselves with diligent, consistent training.

People who make critical thinking a part of their daily lives will learn to formulate their problems clearly and concisely, and will *watch themselves* think about solutions, asking whether the data they're using is relevant, sufficient, and logical. They'll keep asking questions (primarily of themselves!) and test any conclusions they come to against both intellectual standards and their own objectives. They will take great pains to make sure they don't accept faulty interpretations, or fail to consider alternatives. They are simultaneously open-minded and geared toward refining and concluding. They are above all curious and want to find the best way to satisfy this curiosity—not to be "right," but for the satisfaction of cultivating knowledge about themselves and the world. In all this, they don't lose sight of the context in which they operate, and they know how to communicate with others, even in complex situations or where viewpoints differ.

Let's consider a few examples of how this entire process works together. Imagine you're at a get-together of friends and are introduced to someone new, and you strike up a conversation with them. You compliment them on their cool shirt, and they tell you how surprisingly cheap it was and what a good deal they got on it. You make a lighthearted comment about how it was probably made in a sweatshop somewhere, like so much of our clothing today. The other person laughs but says, "Well, let's hope not. But not all sweatshops are bad."

You gear up to disagree and share what you know about the issue: that sweatshops for major clothing labels are responsible for some of the worst human rights violations in the world and exploit third-world countries only to make massive profits for already wealthy corporations. In fact, you're surprised that this person doesn't know this, and soon you're embroiled in a heated discussion.

However, if you were a practiced critical thinker, you would pause and show some humility, becoming genuinely curious about your new friend's position and claims and what information they have to back them up. You would be aware of your own emotional investment in the issue and start to question your own perspective rather than jump in with an argument based on assumptions.

Throughout your conversation, you ask thoughtful but focused questions to understand their point of view—and your own. Why do they think that some sweatshops are not bad? Where did they get their information? You practice fairness in your thinking. You hold off on concluding until you've gathered the facts.

After a lengthy conversation, you discover that this person comes from a country where "sweatshops" pay workers in one week what they'd receive doing a month's worth of any other work. You learn that many previously destitute people can work and support their families because of these clothing manufacturers—and your friend comes from one of these families. You learn that although sweatshops do subject workers to horrific conditions, they also happen to be the best option for many in some countries—complicated information you didn't possess before.

You quickly realize that sweatshops are an issue you've never really taken the time to consider. There's more to it than you thought. You also realize that, compared to your friend, you possess less information about this topic and are not even sure where your impressions about it come from. You leave the conversation with a renewed interest in better understanding your friend's home country's politics and are grateful for the opportunity to have questioned your knee-jerk, unexamined opinions about a very complex topic.

In this example, the elements under question include:

Point of view (how your unique perspective affected your conclusions)

Information (whether you have sufficient knowledge to conclude, or are missing key pieces of information)

Concepts (the popular "zero sum" model of cheap labor in developing countries)

Assumptions (An obvious one: that nobody *wants* to work in a sweatshop, right?)

Intellectual standards can then be applied to these in turn:

Depth and breadth could be applied to your point of view (i.e., is yours really the only viable one?)

You can use some standards for useful information (Is it sufficient and high quality? Where did you get your opinion from?)

You can apply the same standards you have for information to your concepts (Is your model of sweatshops accurate? Does it reflect the reality this other person is sharing with you?)

The standard of accuracy and significance can be applied to the assumptions you've made (Simply, are they true? Have you been focusing on the wrong thing?)

All the above can be considered together with the critical thinking traits of intellectual humility and fair-mindedness (i.e., because winning the argument is not worth offending and alienating your conversation partner.)

Failing to understand the elements of your thinking (your point of view, the data you have, the assumptions) or work hard to improve their quality by applying intellectual standards (asking about the logic, veracity, relevance and depth of your thought processes) may have taken this conversation in a completely different direction. It could have well turned into an argument, especially if instead of challenging your assumptions and realizing you were coming to conclusions based on incomplete data, you assumed the other person was ignorant, and it was your job to educate them.

Though you still think it's not a clever idea to buy "fast fashion," you have a more nuanced understanding of the issue than you did before. Because of your critical thinking, you *learned* something and improved your own intellectual abilities in the process. I'm sure you can agree that is more satisfying overall than the mere feeling of having "won" the argument!

Let's take a look at a more concrete example. As a clothing manufacturer, you're interested in using a newly developed cotton polyester blend that will be cheaper than your current fabric. But you have concerns about its quality and how well it will work with your machines, so you do some trial runs with sample fabric to test factory performance.

Already, you have worked to form a *concept* (an experiment to test the new fabric) from which you intend to draw *inferences* (if it works in the experiment, it will work on a larger scale) for a stated *purpose* (to save money on fabric). To all of these elements of reasoning, you can then apply a few intellectual standards. You ask whether you're being *accurate* in your measurement of the fabric performance. You ask whether the cost of the fabric is truly the only parameter to consider, or whether other things you're not thinking of could jeopardize your stated aim (i.e., you apply questions of *depth* and *breadth*).

You notice that you *want* a particular outcome (you are aware of your own point of view and see how this affects the questions you ask) but try hard to experiment neutrally. When the experiment shows that the new fabric gets jammed in one sewing machine, you use logic to extrapolate to an appropriate conclusion: the fabric is incompatible with one type of machine, but that doesn't logically follow that *every* type of machine will have the same problem. And so it goes.

However, perhaps you notice that not all of the standards have been applied here—for example, the question of *fairness* is not considered, and there is only a very narrow view of the question (lack of *depth* and *breadth*), with an extremely limited understanding of *consequences*. The company may switch to the new fabric, only to discover that it washes poorly and that customers are so unsatisfied with it after purchase that within a few months, repeat custom drops significantly, completely cancelling any small gains made in using the cheaper fabric.

Here, a critical thinker would notice the problem, update their mental model and make a point to remember this the next time they face a decision similar to this one. They would recognize that a few of their underlying premises were not sound—i.e., the idea that the clothing cost and whether it worked with the machines were the *only* parameters to consider.

Critical thinking can be applied on grand scales to big decisions like these or in smaller situations like the conversation we saw at the get-together. You could apply critical thinking every time you use your brain—which, luckily, is pretty much continuously. The first step is to become aware of the various elements of your thinking. Your goals, limitations, the "map" of reality you are using. But the next step is to take responsibility for these elements, and apply intellectual standards to improve them.

Is the way you're thinking clear? Logical? Fair? Are you focusing on the right things, and have you properly understood your goal? Eventually, critical thinking becomes more automatic. This doesn't mean that you are never wrong or that you suddenly become a super-intelligent megamind. Rather, you are taking conscious control of your own mental and intellectual machinery, and using it to its highest potential.

You may still be wrong, you may still feel confused, and you may still miss or misunderstand massive amounts of information out there, even though you explicitly try not to. However, making mistakes for a critical thinker is not a problem—it's merely more "grist for the mill," and can be fed back in and processed again, this time with the privilege of having updated your concepts, sharpened your goals and verified your claims. In essence, critical thinking is not really about *what* you think, but rather *how* you're thinking about it. Focus on improving the quality of the process, and the content of your thoughts will naturally improve as well.

The Laws of Logic

A final element of not trusting your instincts is recognizing how the laws of logic work—or don't—in what you observe, see, and hear. Used correctly, the laws of logic will lead you to the naked truth. Ignored, others will blindfold you.

Like with cognitive biases, the laws of logic go unnoticed by nature. We rarely dissect statements from a logical perspective, making for habitually sloppy arguments and poor understanding. If something *sounds* credible, we deem it credible.

There's a funny, if somewhat cynical, piece of "advice" for people who are a little unsettled about speaking in public: "If you can't dazzle them with brilliance, baffle them with B.S." In this context, "B.S." does *not* stand for "Bachelor of Science."

We've all been in conversations where we realize that the person we're speaking with is saying something *wrong*. For whatever reason, their words don't add up. No matter, they continue, and it causes a cognitive clog in your brain.

They probably think they're making sense—they don't *think* they're trying to baffle you with B.S. But on the other hand, maybe they *are*. They might be trying to convolute your thinking with distorted logic and crazy talk. Whatever the case, you can't quite put your finger on what's rubbing you the wrong way, and thus can't form a rebuttal. They continue to gloat and build their argument on a house of cards.

The problem isn't with your comprehension or ability to think; it's the opposite. You're dealing with someone *defying the laws of logic*, and while your ears are taking it all in, your brain's not having any of it. That's what causes the confusion.

But for the most part, this happens by accident in everyday conversations where the people are well-intentioned. We've all done it before. We get caught up in making a firm point, get flustered if we're not convincing enough, and end up making statements that don't seem to make any sense because they don't. We spitball on earlier statements in an attempt to salvage an argument, and hope they aren't picked apart.

It's beneficial to understand the basic nature of logical thinking and construction. In the world we live, it's a crucial mental skill to develop. It helps us ferret out the truth and process problems. It imparts the ability to parse arguments and statements and know if they need to be dealt with. This is one of Aristotle's main legacies to the world.

As a quick example, a friend may be trying to remember the shoes they were wearing a particular day. They say, "If I was wearing sandals, they were red." So far, so good. They go on to say, "I'm pretty sure my shoes were red, which means I was wearing sandals." Well, that second part doesn't follow—hopefully, an alarm has been set off in your brain. It doesn't logically add up, and you're about to learn why.

Dissecting logical arguments sounds complicated, but the foundation of logical thinking is pretty easy to understand. The concepts are straightforward. They use sentence structure and equations to illustrate how arguments are or are not sound at their core. Understanding them breaks down to assessing the distinct kinds of statements people make in explaining a concept or an argument. Here, we will go over four of the most often used laws of logical statements—two of which are *il*logical!

Conditional statements: X -> Y. The first of our so-called laws of logic is the conditional statement. It is simply a true statement to be taken at face value. We'll use a conditional statement as the core example for all these arguments— "If you feed my dog kibbles, then he'll be friendly to you." To make things easy to understand, let's assume in this discussion that this statement is *always* true. There is a causal relationship.

This is called a conditional statement because it says, "*If* this condition is met, *then* this result will one hundred percent happen." The condition is your feeding your friend's dog kibbles. The result is that the dog will be friendly to you. There is a direct cause and effect relationship between the condition and the result, and it only functions in one direction—there has been no cause and effect relationship established backward.

Once again, we're pretending this will always be the case—every time you give this dog a kibble, he's going to love you. Using this as a given, the statement is logically sound.

We also call the relationship between the condition and the result one of *premise* and *conclusion*—broader terms that can be used for other statements. If a particular premise is true, you can expect the conclusion or outcome to be true.

These types of statements generally don't present as issues unless someone is trying to pass off that the conclusion will always be true when it isn't. It's when you start to play with it that problems arise.

Converse statements: Y -> X. Now, consider this statement: "If my dog is friendly to you, it is because you fed him kibbles."

Is this true, given what we learned about conditional statements? If "If you feed my dog kibbles, then he'll be friendly to you" *(X -> Y)* is true, does that mean the reverse is necessarily true? Well—it's certainly a *possibility*, since we've determined that feeding the dog kibbles is a surefire way to win his friendliness. But is it the *only* way to make the dog friendly? Maybe you petted him. Perhaps you spoke to him in a gentle, friendly tone of voice. Perhaps you played a game of fetch with him that made him extremely happy, and he returned his happiness with intense affection to you. Maybe the dog is in a good mood. Dogs do that.

In short, no, *Y -> X* is often a flawed argument—an illogical statement.

This is an example of a converse statement: it reverses the conclusion and the premise, or the result and the condition—it says that the prerequisite is true if the result is true. And it's turned the statement into a logical flaw. Feeding the dog kibbles will indeed make him your friend. But there's no indication that he's friends with you strictly because you fed him kibbles. There are other ways you can make a dog friendly to you. You've just caught someone with their hand in the cookie jar. Remember, a statement only has cause and effect in one direction—from condition to result, and not the other way around.

A converse statement is the direct parent of something called the *false syllogism*—basically, a false premise. Its fallacy is also exposed in making leaps of judgment based on misunderstood connections, like this:

Dogs love kibbles.

Monkeys love kibbles.

Therefore, dogs are monkeys.

In this statement, the two premises might be true. But the fact that both dogs and monkeys like kibbles doesn't mean they're the same thing. The premise used for establishing the conclusion—mutual kibble love—is therefore false, as is the conclusion. Converse statements are where you'll catch people the most, because the cause and effect relationship isn't always closely examined.

Inverse statements: Not X -> Not Y. Okay, let's try this one on for size: "If you *don't* feed my dog kibbles, then he *won't* be friendly to you."

Really? That's the dog you have? If I don't feed him kibbles—if I've run out or, you know, just don't carry kibbles on me out of habit—then he's going to turn on me? What an ingrate.

This is an inverse statement. It preserves the premise-conclusion relationship of the original statement but turns it into a *negative*: "If this doesn't happen, then this won't happen as a result." It assumes a deeper relationship between the two than exists.

Cause and effect certainly doesn't work if the lack of a cause means the lack of an effect.

Inverse statements are trickier because not all of them are wrong. Sometimes they're right: "If you don't brush your teeth, then they won't be healthy." Well, that's true. But it leaves out that there are other ways to make your teeth unhealthy—constantly eating food that's bad for your teeth, for example (even if you do brush).

It could very well be that the dog rejects all who do not bring him kibbles. I don't know this particular dog's neurosis when it comes to being fed kibbles at the appropriate time; I suppose it may turn him into a hostile, nervous wreck.

Still, the dog may be unfriendly for other reasons. Maybe he just got back from chasing a car he didn't catch, so he's a little disappointed. Maybe he's in a bad mood. Maybe you've insulted him. Maybe he was recently neutered. There are plenty of things that can tick this dog off besides kibble deprivation.

So, while certain inverse statements might be right, not all of them will be. Be extra cautious with them, and don't take them at face value. Many things will try to pass themselves off as true statements, but you can begin to see that most of them are logical flaws.

Contrapositive statements: Not Y -> Not X. These are statements that negate both the premise and the conclusion, both backward and forward. If the original conditional statement is correct, then the contrapositive is also always true, unlike the converse or inverse statements. This type of relationship exists both ways, because it's about a negative.

In our trusty dog food analogy, the conditional is "If you give the dog kibbles, then he will be friendly," and the contrapositive would be "If my dog is unfriendly to you, then you didn't give him kibbles." This is true. This is *always* true. There could be many reasons why the dog is being a jerk (see above). But one thing's for sure: if he's unfriendly, then for sure you haven't given him any of his cure-all kibbles. If you did, the dog would be more agreeable. But he isn't, so you haven't. Remember, that part is a given, so if the result is not true, then the given is also not true.

Another quick example: if you go swimming, you will be wet. What does the contrapositive statement sound like? If you are not wet, you did not go swimming. That certainly seems to make sense.

It can take a bit to decipher these types of logical statements, but once you do, you'll find that you can understand the truth of matters instantly. Our instincts make us want to skip over the details of these statements because they make sense on the surface. It's almost as if our instincts are working against us these days!

Summary:

- Practical intelligence is another way of saying common sense, but we all know that common sense truly is not so common. One of the key lessons to learn with practical intelligence is that nothing is what it seems at first glance. The world doesn't readily reveal itself nakedly to you, so it's up to you to look beneath the surface to understand what you see. We want to do this, but we are too often driven by certainty and speed instead of actual truth.

- The first and most natural way to probe below the surface is through cultivating curiosity. There are five types of curiosity, each of which can be a motivation for asking questions: joyous exploration, deprivation sensitivity, stress tolerance, social curiosity, and thrill-seeking. However, curiosity will rarely come easily or naturally, especially about things we don't have an innate interest in. So, we need to generate that same approach through other methods.

- One methodical way to seek truth and simulate curiosity is by embracing skepticism. No, it's not about being *cynical* or simply refusing to believe what people tell you. Rather, it's refusing to blindly believe what people tell you and requiring evidence and facts. In this way, a skeptic is quite similar to a scientist utilizing the scientific method. No answer is required here, and only understanding is sought. Skepticism requires slowing down your thoughts and thinking like a scientist.

- Next, we come to critical thinking. Critical thinking is concerned with questioning answers rather than asking questions. It seeks to take nothing at face value and provide a three-dimensional and nuanced view of a topic or stance. Without that, you are by definition jumping to conclusions or relying on someone else's word—an opinion without inquiry is a weak one. We can practice critical thinking through a series of questions, but we can also go deeper by running inquiries and thoughts through the

Paul-Elder framework of critical thinking. This involves three components that ultimately work together to build a bulletproof thinking process: (1) elements of thought and reasoning, (2) intellectual standards to be applied to these elements, and (3) the cultivation and eventual development of intellectual traits.

- Finally, it's important to understand logical arguments—especially *illogical* arguments. This is how you determine the truth and validity of what is being said. We hear these every day but may not pick out their logical flaws. You can think of these as a combination of math and argumentation. There is the conditional statement (X -> Y, true), the converse statement (Y -> X, usually a flaw), the inverse statement (Not X -> Not Y, usually a flaw), and the contrapositive statement (Not Y -> Not X, true). It's not just word games; it's understanding the foundations upon which true and misleading arguments are built.

Chapter 4: Freedom from the Demands of Others

So far in this book, we've been questioning the unspoken assumption that our brains are neutral, computer-like entities that accurately appraise the world around us and make objective decisions about it. In chapter 2, we considered how our perceptions and our cognitions could be heavily influenced or even completely determined by peers or the social influences that surround us on every side. To be an independent thinker means being aware of these effects and doing what it takes to work against them.

But it's probably becoming clear that there are not just cognitive, intellectual threats to clear and independent thought. Human beings are also social, emotional, and even spiritual creatures guided by our thinking and feelings. And we don't merely feel in isolated, discrete ways within ourselves, but we feel *with* other people. Without empathy, compassion, and cooperation, we would lose our humanity in a very tangible way.

However, being enmeshed and engrossed in the feeling worlds of others is something that can understandably jeopardize our ability to think and feel for ourselves. Being an independent thinker is not just a simple matter of sitting in a quiet room and teasing out a nice, clean, logical line of reasoning. No matter how "pure" of thought, nobody can escape the fact that they live in a world with others. This world has pronounced moral and ethical elements; it's a world where family obligations and commitments exist, compromises are often necessary, and being "kind" and "correct" are not always the same.

The question, then, becomes

Where do my thoughts begin and the other person's end?

What is my intention, and what is a demand or expectation placed on me by others?

What is my personal perception and judgment, and what is my acknowledgment of other peoples'?

As you can see, this balancing act is not just a philosophical and intellectual exercise but a psychological and relational one. In other words, being an independent thinker (and feeler) means having healthy boundaries.

Setting and Enforcing Boundaries

If you were to read a review of yourself, perhaps in an appraisal at work, you might be pleased to see yourself described as "accommodating" and "agreeable." This might be a good review at work, but are they generally good words to be described with? Be careful, as you might be fooled with the misplaced positivity around them.

To be accommodating or agreeable means adapting to make others happy, which isn't establishing boundaries—it's a distinct lack of assertiveness.

It's not bad to be agreeable, and often this comes from a place of empathy—a psychological desire to create social harmony and to make life better for everyone else. By itself, it's a positive force and neutral at worst. But it's the way that you might allow yourself to blur your lines in the name of agreeableness that it becomes a negative force in your life.

Agreeableness can also come from a desire to be liked, resulting in a lack of genuineness and self suppression. In an interesting display of the complexity of human nature, most people are annoyed by people-pleasing.

In a 2010 study published in the *Journal of Personality and Social Psychology*, researchers analyzed people's reactions to selfish versus generous actions in a game about rewards. Instead of appreciating the generous players, they found that these were equally disliked as the selfish ones.

The unselfish members who gave toward the provision of a public good but used little of it themselves were also excluded from the group. Two follow-up studies were conducted, which found it wasn't unpredictability or confusion causing these results. People just found the generous players as unlikeable as the selfish ones.

It seemed that these agreeable players made other people feel bad about themselves. They were also deemed "rule-breakers." Although they were breaking the rules of negative social norms positively, it was too much. Trying to be too nice, whether to impress or craving for social harmony, actually caused people to exclude them from the very group they wanted to help.

You may have tried taking on the dirty jobs nobody else wants or paying a bar tab at a work party in the hope it would endear you to a group. This is likely to have the opposite effect; your extreme generosity makes people just as uncomfortable as the selfish people who make life more difficult or refuse to contribute.

Going against the grain, even if that's by doing charitable deeds, makes you stand out as a target. You're just as likely as the selfish person to be recommended for *voluntary redundancy* or to find there never seems to be room for you in any of the cars on road trips.

University of Notre Dame researchers in 2011 found that disagreeable employees earned more than their agreeable counterparts. Disagreeable men earned eighteen percent more than agreeable men. Agreeableness is a more socially expected norm in women, but disagreeable women still earned five percent more than the agreeable women, and these agreeable women lagged far behind the disagreeable men.

Agreeable people do just that: they agree, don't rock the boat, and don't dare to tread potentially controversial topics like pay raises or higher starting salaries. Agreeing to everything is a sure path to becoming a pushover.

The agreeable employee has a huge workload causing him sleepless nights. He's approached by five colleagues asking for support and agreed to help them all. They've talked, wondering what he does all day if he's got time to help everyone. His boss makes yet another unreasonable demand, and he accepts it, disguising his impending doom at how he will get it all done.

Another colleague refuses to help others, and when asked the same question demands, he is paid more for it and is promoted to a managerial position because he's often asked for advice. The boss agrees to his demands and delegates some of his workloads to the agreeable employee.

Since childhood, most people are told to be kind, put others first, and try to make life run smoothly; the playground peacemaker grows up to be the office diplomat. Being accommodating, agreeable, and selfless leads to being undervalued and even excluded from a group. This seems unfair but likely rings true with experiences you've had in your life.

There is something else at work behind the compulsion to be agreeable and accommodating. It seems that other people don't always view these traits as positive or pleasurable to be around. When we avoid assertiveness, we don't want to appear rude or selfish, but you're making a bad impression when you appear selfless and altruistic. It's in your best interest to assert your rights and boundaries and look after number one.

Choosing and Enforcing Your Boundaries

A boundary is an invisible barrier that surrounds your personal space. This definition includes physical space—the immediate, literal area around you—and emotional space. We're interested in the emotional kind.

Boundaries set the limits of how much people can trespass into your emotional life. They regulate the "space" you need to be your true self with no duress, which you need other people to respect.

With sound boundaries, you feel freer to be yourself without the burden of others' expectations or demands. At the same time, a reasonable boundary lets you invite whom *you* want to share your emotions with—after, of course, you've defined your boundaries based on your needs.

It can be difficult to acknowledge when others invade our personal space and overstep our limits. After all, you've projected yourself as someone who's there for everyone all the time without any regard for your necessities. Other people's obligations are inside your boundaries for all intents and purposes. If that's the case, then what is the point? So, the first step in setting up healthy boundaries is understanding *when* that line is being crossed and what it *feels* like when it happens.

To do that, you can start by paying attention to your body and mind. How does your body react when you're around someone who's troubling you or wearing you out? Some typical symptoms might be a clenching of the gut or tension in your head. Also, explain what goes through your mind when you're around this person—is it confused, inattentive, or racing with ideas on how to get away? What small signs of unhappiness might you be experiencing regularly? You may not be able to recognize violated boundaries in the moment, but the aftermath should be fairly telling. You'll know how tense or unhappy you feel after an interaction.

After that diagnosis, you'll have some time to define exactly what it is about this person that upsets you. Is it in their character (are they abrasive, hyperactive, unthinking)? Are they more direct than you're comfortable with? Do they say things to offend or annoy you? Be honest and unsparing with yourself—

remember, you don't have to share this information with anybody else.

With all the information you've just gathered—your physical reaction, mental reaction, and problem with the person—you've produced an alarm system. If you've ingested all these steps faithfully, the next time you sense any of those things happening, they'll serve as a warning that you need to reexamine or set boundaries.

Here's an example. Alexa and Elena are sisters. Elena had just introduced her boyfriend, Daniel, to the family. Daniel started coming to family functions for a few months, and gradually Alexa found herself hanging out with Daniel more often.

But something happened when Alexa was around Daniel. Her stomach got upset when Daniel asked her a question. Her mind got cluttered. Her nerves reacted, and she felt inclined to flee. But she didn't want to tell Daniel off because she'd possibly tick off Elena and cause a family ruckus.

After Alexa thought about how she reacted around Daniel, she realized he seemed curiously over-interested in other people's private lives—specifically, the romantic parts. Daniel was uncommonly frank in their conversations and sometimes asked for personal details that went too far. And he did so pleasantly as if every family in the world has these kinds of conversations freely and openly. He didn't realize his questions were causing tension. But they drove Alexa, a very private person, up the wall. Alexa diagnosed the situation and decided to set some boundaries.

Sure enough, the next time they were together, Daniel started interrogating Alexa about her online dating history. (Alexa had told Elena she'd sworn off online dating for good, which Elena must have told Daniel.) Alexa, very calmly, told Daniel, "Look, I've been giving this much thought, and I don't feel comfortable discussing my private life in that much detail. I know you don't mean harm, and I appreciate your friendliness, but I'm asking you to respect my limits in this matter."

Daniel was taken aback. He had no idea his questions weren't appropriate. He mumbled an apology and walked away. He never asked Alexa anything again. Elena's relationship with Daniel lasted for about eight months after the confrontation. While Alexa never cozied up to Daniel in a meaningful way, they did manage a civil and friendly rapport with each other until the breakup, after which Alexa never saw him again.

It could have been worse: Daniel could have gotten angry, Elena could have gotten upset, and the family could have suffered a big fallout. But whatever the outcome was, Alexa rightfully issued a statement that she had to stand her ground and construct a boundary.

Sometimes there will be fallout from setting boundaries, especially among those who are oblivious as opposed to malicious. But the fallout is almost always worth it—look at the tradeoff Alexa made. Though it may be difficult for you to see at the moment with emotions running high, it's not even close.

Now it's time to do some serious self-investigation and come up with a firm set of boundaries that'll help you curb your addiction to a lack of assertion. Here are some processes that will help you along.

Determine your core values. Life can be so hectic that you don't have much time for knowing who you are and what you value. Some of us never have that introspection, even when we have time to do so. Sometimes, when we think about what we believe or value, we may only think about what others tell us to believe or value—our religious beliefs, cultures, or traditions.

It's essential to put all that aside for a little while and concentrate on what *you*, the person, really esteem and what makes up your individual personal code. To figure that out, think of things that make you uncomfortable in some way and how they cause you to act. They don't have to be huge, important, or even significant things. They can just be events that happen regularly enough for you to notice them.

For example, Howard couldn't deal with paying an exorbitant amount of money for a parking spot. It didn't align with his values (or, probably more to the point, what he could afford). But he lived near a big city where he went to professional sporting events, where parking spots regularly cost almost $100 for six hours. No way Howard was dealing with that. Instead, he drove to a park-and-ride and took the light rail to the game for $5 per round-trip.

Fascinating story, I know. But even this rather slight tale offers a couple of ideas about Howard's values:

He's frugal, at least when it comes to parking spaces.

He's fine with taking "the long way" if he needs to.

He supports public transit.

I call those statements "surface values," because they're just a series of indicators as to what

Howard's *core* values might be. By doing a little reverse-engineering, we can come up with examples of Howard's potential core values:

financial responsibility

patience

public-mindedness

Try this mental exercise on some of the things *you* do. Take a situation, routine, or event in your life, think about how you act in it, and try to relate them to the values you have. You might find some values you weren't completely aware of. Come up with as many examples as you can—eventually, a few core values will keep popping up more than others, and those are probably the ones you *really* believe in.

Here's one important thing to remember: when you're doing this exercise and the event you're analyzing involves your relationship with someone else, make sure you focus on *your* values and what makes *you* comfortable or uneasy. Don't consider what the *other person* might value or frame your values in the context of the relationship. You have permission to be self-centered in this procedure. Achieve a firm understanding of what you stand for.

Change yourself—and only yourself. While reaffirming your values and getting ready to set boundaries, you might think to yourself, *'This situation would be better if my friends/partners/parents/children/coworkers would accept my way of thinking. If everybody could see it my way, there'd be no problem at all.'*

It's human to want that. When we come across a solution, we want to tell everybody about how we've fixed ourselves: "I was messed up! I'm not messed up anymore! You're still messed up! You need to do exactly what I did!"

Or maybe we just want people to stop being so hard to deal with. We want our partners to stop being lazy around the house; our bosses to stop belittling us; our friends to quit being melodramatic. That's human, too.

But we're not responsible for changing the behaviors of others. Not only that, but it's simply not under our control or up to us. What you *can* and should change is how you *deal* with other people. You're not going to stop people from attempting to violate your boundaries, but you can change how you deal with these attempts.

This means changing your approach based on those core values we've just discovered and acting in a way that communicates boundaries. It means communicating differently with people you're having issues with. It also means standing your emotional ground with people who are being overly aggressive with your personal space.

Let's say someone you're close with is a compulsive over-spender. They're always buying things they don't need. They occasionally ask for loans but always seem to have a lot of stuff or go on vacations more than a broke person should.

You know, if this person would just adopt more stringent budgeting practices, they'd change their ways. If only they paid closer attention to their bank balance or got better at planning their financial future, just like you have. In fact, you're going to march over to this person's apartment with a copy of *Budgeting for Dummies*, and you're going to tell them their lifestyle is a highway to financial insolvency and bankruptcy—right?

Well, no. You're not responsible for this person's problems. You do not have the time to spend fixing them. You have your things to deal with. But what you *can* do is not give them money anymore. You can only change your behavior to not enable or support other people's behaviors. You are only a part of someone else's mental calculus.

Altering how you deal with others is a much more rewarding exercise than converting people to your way of thinking. Anytime you can work on your initiative and do something transformative for yourself, it'll be much more effective and fruitful for your health.

Set the consequences. So, what happens after somebody's ignored your limits and happily trespassed into your personal space after you've told them to respect your boundaries?

The answer: whatever you want. Within reason, that is. You're not entitled to start a street fight or hack their computer. But you *are* entitled to stand your emotional ground and defend your personal space in a way that your message gets heard. To do that, you have to decide what the consequence will be when someone goes past your boundaries. The only thing you're not allowed to do is *nothing*.

For example, let's say there's someone on Facebook who's continually hounding you about a dispute they're having. You've offered warnings to him about pestering you in a public forum, but he keeps doing it. So, you decide upon the consequence of unfriending or blocking him from your feed.

This part can be a big, hard step for you emotionally. It's an anxious moment. Still, it's part of setting your boundaries. This is about *your* needs and yours alone. Those are the needs you have to respect. If someone's crossing that threshold continually despite your admonitions for them to stop, you have to lay down the law for yourself.

You can expect them to react unfavorably, of course. They might call you judgmental, short-sighted, unfair, rash, or irrational. *Count* on them being that way. Simply consider it part of the process of setting the consequence. But don't let it change your decision.

Another great step to take when setting consequences is writing them down ahead of time. I recommend writing things down for pretty much any situation, but it's especially good to do here. Write down the boundaries you have, the actions others might take that trespass those boundaries, and exactly *what* you will do when they've violated your boundaries. Writing is good for organizing your thoughts and reminding you what you've decided if you need to in the future. It's often difficult to make sound decisions when we're emotional or fearful, so knowing what we've previously decided with a clear mind can help us act.

Having a firm policy about the consequences of going over your limits helps you develop more resolve and self-respect.

Get clear and specific on what your boundaries are. You're the one who decides what will work for you and what won't. When setting up and explaining your boundaries, you have to be as explicit and direct as you can about them. It's impossible to get someone to respect your boundaries if you're not clear on them yourself. For example, if you don't know that you resent people eating at your dining room table and leaving a mess behind, how will *they*?

You're allowed to make different boundaries for different people in your life. Not everybody has to follow the same slate of rules and regulations; they can vary according to how close certain people might be to you. It's one thing when a family member or close friend asks if they can borrow your car, but it's quite another when a casual buddy from work or the bar does so. If you need to adjust the boundaries for some and not others, that's your call.

Finally, people might not understand why you've set up certain limitations, rules, or boundaries. That's completely okay. They don't have to. They're your decisions. If other people don't understand that or feel that your rules go against *their* emotions or values, it matters not one bit. Don't worry about 'em.

Communicate your boundaries to others in very exact terms. Make sure everybody's truly clear on what your limits are (especially if they're different for various people). You must be clear, candid, and forthright with others about what your boundaries are. You can't assume they'll just guess correctly.

For example, people keep crashing on your sofa. Every weekend, someone you know stays out late and doesn't want to drive back to their home for whatever reason. So, they knock on your door, ask if they can crash, you back down, and 15 minutes later, your sofa's closed for the night. And there's also a fair chance they'll sneak something from your fridge while you're asleep. It takes personal space away and probably eats a bit of your time as well.

You probably haven't made it expressly clear that this arrangement no longer works for you. You haven't set this boundary clearly, preferring to passive-aggressively hint that you're annoyed and prefer not to have this happen. So, they'll keep doing it because they don't know you have a problem with it. Until you state without equivocation what your boundaries are, folks are going to keep traipsing right through them.

Some people will get it if you just drop a slight hint. For example, take that story about Alexa and Daniel, the guy who asked too-personal questions. Alexa may have expressed her boundaries by simply responding, "Why do you ask?" Many people will pick up on that clue and back off, leaving your boundaries intact.

Others aren't quite as intuitive, and if they keep on not taking the hint, then it's time for you to be explicit and direct with them. This is the tough part. Alexa could have said something like "I don't like to discuss that," "I'm not going to do that," or "Please stop harping on me about this topic." That magic word "no" is a direct way to defend your boundaries. Similarly, to defend your couch, you can offer, "This isn't going to work for me anymore," or "This is the last time you'll be able to do this without X," or just, "This isn't going to happen again."

If someone doesn't understand your set of boundaries and questions you why you have them in place, you are not required to answer them. You don't owe any explanation. You don't have to describe your reasoning or what caused you to make that decision. You don't have to justify a thing. You know yourself, and you know what's important to you. You know why you feel the way you do. That is all you need to be concerned about. You don't have to draw a diagram for anybody else. Remember, when communicating your boundaries, "no" is a complete sentence.

Don't let boundary-crossers off the hook. You've figured out your boundaries. You've clearly explained them to others. You've defined what the consequences will be. And yet, someone's still going past your limits. So, what now?

You have to lay down your personal law and not let the violators off easy. It's time to act.

Implementing your personal boundaries is necessary when trying to establish your limits and assert yourself. That's why *you should only set rules that you are willing to carry out*. Any regulation you set that you're only going to enforce halfway is probably one you should reconsider—you either don't really feel the limit is necessary or you haven't quite worked out all the details. People will take notice and take it as a sign that you aren't serious about your boundaries—they might as well not exist at that point. This is known as a *porous boundary*, and it's a sign of weakness that people will immediately exploit.

Some folks will resent your setting down limits and dishing out consequences. We'll go a little more into detail about how to contend with more negative outcomes in just a little bit, but for now, know that it will happen.

For example, it would have been easy to simply try and not let your Facebook bully friend bug you. You could have ignored him or found other ways to deal with him. But you know if you allow him to continue to have that access to you, he's only going to keep doing what he does. You've explained yourself, you've defined your limits, and he's ignored them. Hit that "unfriend" button and don't look back.

If you back up your boundaries with solid action, you'll find that there'll be only a small bit of anxiety in the action itself—far less than there would be if you keep letting it fester.

You now know how to define your boundaries, explain them, and enforce them. And you also know that boundary rules can be different according to whom you're dealing with. Now, let's discuss what actually happens when people cross over into your personal space, whether they're invited or not.

When you're involved in an interaction with someone, there are three levels that depict how deeply you're protecting your boundaries. Simply put, there's too strong, too weak, and just right.

Healthy. The goal is to maintain your boundaries in a balanced manner. A healthy boundary will reinforce your character, moderate your emotional reactions, and help you be generous in a meaningful way.

When you have healthy boundaries, you have a healthy respect for yourself, your feelings, and your viewpoint. You don't sell out your core values so others can take advantage of them. You exchange and reveal personal information suitably and properly. You're also able to handle it when people say no to you.

Rigid. You can also be extra-firm when setting your boundaries and turn yourself into an impenetrable fortress. But there are serious drawbacks to this approach. You're likely to have few if any intimate or close relationships with anyone. You'll appear distant and removed from other people, possibly isolated. You'll be reticent to ask anyone else for assistance, and you'll keep yourself away from vulnerable situations, so you don't have to deal with rejection.

The rigid boundary-setter does everything possible to avoid being exposed, weak, or too available because they don't want to get hurt by anybody else. But in doing so, they still get hurt—by themselves.

Porous. Someone with very thin boundaries tends to let a lot of people and forces into their life to basically act out their will. When you keep porous boundaries, you tend to give out too much personal information or get far too involved in the problems of other people. "No" is a word you have an extremely challenging time saying. You open yourself up to discourteous and abusive people—in fact, you practically invite and permit people to take advantage of your goodwill.

The porous boundary-setter is far too trusting and unreserved about other people. They get exploited regularly, even by people with no intentions to exploit them. They're often disappointed and can become bitter about their existence even as they still over-share themselves. This is another way of describing blurry boundaries.

Looking over this information, you're probably inclined to believe that the healthy level is the one you should shoot for 100% of the time. That's not a terrible starting place. But you *will* find that you might need to adjust in either direction depending on certain factors.

For example, if you have a good relationship with your family, most likely you'd be a little more porous to them. If you're in a working relationship with someone you mistrust, you'd probably nudge yourself toward the rigid policy.

You have the freedom to decide how far you'll bend or expand your boundaries in a given situation. But there are very few, if any, situations where it's a good idea to be full-on rigid or porous. Thick-bordered people are hard to reach, are very defensive, and practically walk around in spiky body armor. Thin-bordered ones are overly open and frequently naïve—they're easy to get close to, but their naked sincerity can let bad forces in.

When you're setting your boundaries, the main thing to consider is that you're the one in charge. You have to trust in yourself and believe that what you need, want, and cherish is right. And you have to know that your feelings are equally as important as anyone else's.

When you finally take the personal initiative to respect yourself and set and defend your boundaries, it may bend a few people out of shape. They won't be happy. They'll be upset and maybe sad. A few of them might be pissed off. But staying firm to your boundaries will *help* your relationships and alliances over the long haul.

If someone else's response makes you let down your boundaries, you're going to feel irritated with them as time goes on. You can't let yourself be deterred by them. You need a situation where your friends, relations, and associates truly esteem you for who you are and will respect your limits—even if they feel a little let down or unhappy with your decision at first.

Like any good business plan, you have to account for a certain measure of risk to make your boundary settings more likely to succeed. In this case, you have to allow for the possibility—in fact, fully anticipate—that someone might be angry when you set your boundaries.

You, therefore, need to steel your resolve with someone who might be unreasonably mad with you. You can't accept their bullying or their attempts to break your limits. You can't let them continue to exploit your sympathy or helpfulness or show disdain for the boundaries that are completely your right to establish.

If you allow an angry person to weaken your determination because they scare you, your situation will not improve. Realize this as quickly as you can. By withdrawing your request that they respect your limits, you'll only get more depressed and displeased. In time, that turns into full-on acrimony and hatred.

On the other hand, if you stand firm in the face of someone's indignation with you, the discomfort will only be temporary. They may continue to feel resentful, but you'll at least know that you've stood your ground and defended what's important to you. At least *you* will eventually feel confident that you've made the right choice. Chances are their anger will die down as well, and you'll still have a relationship you can build back up again.

Whatever's making them so angry isn't your problem—it's *theirs*. Once again, you're responsible only for your actions and deeds. *They* are responsible for *their own* reactions. If you sustain an even temperament and hold firm to your convictions about boundaries, maybe they'll finally learn they need to respect others more often.

Don't take an angry person's bait. If their rage is starting to careen out of control, keep yourself calm. Don't let them dictate the hostile tone of the exchange just because they're infuriated. This is one of those rare situations where remaining idle is a sign of strength. Let them storm their head off and quietly go about your business.

You might be tempted in the presence of an angry person to immediately try and make them feel better and get back in their good graces. But you should resist the urge to make it all better as well, because you'll still be ceding your power to someone who's just going to consume it.

When dealing with the fire and fury of someone angry with your decisions, including those in which you establish your boundaries, the solution is marvelously simple: do nothing. It's not always easy, but it's almost always the best way.

Unfortunately, you will almost always have some sort of negative reaction to your boundaries. This is something you have to prepare for, but it will be difficult, nonetheless. People don't like getting told no, but that reflects on them, not you as a person.

Toxic Takers

Unfortunately, many unhealthy people, relationships, and behaviors don't come from a place of innocence or goodwill. The toxic taker (TT) is a drain that particularly damages unassertive people. It's the TTs who'll be annoyed and upset once you start practicing assertiveness. We may have discussed how to set solid and impermeable boundaries, but sometimes, people are set on violating them regardless.

There will be people in your life who have a warped sense of entitlement. What you've worked for becomes a free resource they can tap into: they demand a job at your office or introductions to others in your field. They ask you to make them a website for free overnight or use your recruitment knowledge to create their CV.

TTs know your every skill and strength but not a single vulnerability other than your need to say yes: they take from you and return nothing, passing off your work as their own or belittling you to others.

Having grown accustomed to the one-sidedness of the relationship, TTs know how insecure you are, so they never consider paying you back or doing something for you. This sends the message that you're less important than them, and people take advantage of you. The feelings of anger, resentment, and disapproval that arise from this spill over into all areas of your life.

The TT wears many disguises. They could be your colleague, sibling, best friend, neighbor, customer, client, teacher, or acquaintance. The TT needs you to help them—not once or twice, but always. Every encounter involves them sharing with you their latest mistakes, admitting their flaws and weaknesses, and regaling you with tales of the latest disaster that's currently destroying their life.

This is deliberate. Being so open and upfront about their shortcomings endears the TT to you. They ensure there's never time to talk about anything other than themselves and lead you down a path of sob stories and manipulation to get what they want. You're never invited to share your problems but always listen to theirs, go out of your way to help them, and lend them money.

The truth is that most TTs harbor a lot of resentment for the people they take from. This stems from complex emotions surrounding their dependence on you and resentment that you don't seem to have their worries. They may believe that it's easy for you, and you owe it to them to help. You taking an interest in their problems may be the only validation they get.

Even the most independent person falls on hard times and must ask for help. You might always want to support the TT because you feel sorry for how often this happens to them. The difference is that things never seem to improve for the TT. If one problem seems to be taken care of, in swoops another one to take its place. The money you lent wasn't enough; the problem was more complex than they first thought. TTs never manage to remove themselves fully from the problematic situation. They're also not afraid to invent disasters to extract more from you.

There are two ways to identify and deal with a TT. The first method is that when they come to you with a problem, sympathize with them but don't offer any help: no solutions, no money, no advice. Just say, "Yes, that does sound terrible."

This is going to require willpower because the TT will continue to elaborate to provoke your natural caregiving response of wanting to solve the problem. It's hard to listen to their heartbreaking speech and resist the urge to jump in with advice or to be the savior. Just keep sympathizing and stop yourself if you want to say more. Make a statement and repeat their feelings ad nauseam.

The TT may seem to give up, but they're going to try to talk to you again about it. You not offering your usual money or assistance is going to disorient them. When they talk to you, they fully expect you to help them and won't expect you to have seen through their act. You have the power of surprise on your side.

They'll become frustrated and annoyed, but even a TT knows when they're beaten, and they'll be off to see who else they can manipulate.

When a TT comes to you with a problem, the second method is to sympathize without offering solutions as above, but then tell them a problem of your own.

TTs don't hang around in packs—there's only room for one victim in their life, and it's not going to be you. When faced with your problem, they'll appear put out and disinterested. You'll probably enjoy watching their attempts at showing empathy. Having broken the number one rule—that is, TTs come first, and you're their assistant—they'll regard you as someone who no longer serves a purpose for them.

The speed at which these methods can cause a TT to disappear from your life may surprise you.

When a TT realizes you have your own problems and can't be their constant life support, they'll stop wasting their time on you. If they value the relationship you had, then they may come back, but they may not want a relationship where their crises don't make them special.

Once the initial shock of you not providing a solution or having your own problems wears off, you can see what happens after. If the TT loses all interest in you once you stop helping them, you'll know exactly where you stand.

Equipped with the two methods to repel TTs, you can begin to look out for the red flags that let you know who isn't looking for a fair, two-way relationship. There are four common examples of TTs that you might recognize from your own life.

The first type of TT is someone who won't say hello without an ulterior motive. A colleague who sometimes turns up at your desk with coffee and a smile might baffle you when she blanks you at a social event until you remember she only ever came to say hi when she needed your help with the printer or some filing.

The second type of TT is the person who won't reciprocate unless forced to. You have lunch with a neighbor once a month, and you paid the first time, but then when the bill came at the second lunch, they directed the waiter to you, and you paid again. You meet for this month's lunch and find you've forgotten your wallet. Your neighbor pays, but you can tell they're not happy about it. When you go to pencil next month's date in your diary, they tell you they're pretty booked up for the rest of the year.

The third type of TT is the person who requires a payment or quid pro quo for them to help you. You ask your new partner to pick up some onions on the way to your apartment for the meal you're making, and they ask you to transfer them the money. You laugh, assuming they're joking, but when they arrive, they ask you for the exact change. When you needed them to pick you up on their way home and drop you along their normal route, they asked you for gas money as if they were going out of their way.

The fourth type of TT is the person who doesn't ask about you or really care. You could recite your best friend's birthday, recent weight gain, bank balance, latest disappointment, and enemies. When they invite you over on a Tuesday, you're surprised as they know you have evening classes—at least you thought they did, until they innocently say, "An evening class? That doesn't sound like you. Why are you starting that?" You spill your heart out about a problem you haven't been able to share with anyone else, and you look over and see them smiling at their phone. They notice you looking and say, "That sounds great. Well done, you."

TTs are tiring and always want more. They have a great eye for identifying accommodating and agreeable people who don't know their rights. TTs prey on generous people-pleasers and won't stop taking until their victim either stops offering solutions or wants to talk about their problems.

Although they must be condemned for taking advantage of your weakness, TTs do serve a purpose in highlighting how your people-pleasing compulsions aren't respected or deserved by others.

If you feel any hint of people-pleasing habits, you must be aware of what can lie in your path. You've read about manipulating behavior, people who will repeatedly violate your boundaries, and even TTs who are out to get you. Even if you are assertive, it doesn't mean you are immunized from these people. You can begin to understand that there is more than meets the eye to being "nice" and agreeable and realize even more why assertiveness is an essential life skill.

Summary:

- We tend to think being agreeable and accommodating are positive traits. They are, but only to a certain extent. Studies have shown that too much of either conveys a negative impression to others—precisely what you want to prevent by not asserting yourself. Thus, it seems to make more sense to assert yourself consistently and stop the need for people-pleasing.
- Strong and clear boundaries will be one of your best defenses against people-pleasing and the people who would have you do so.

However, they can't exist solely in your head, and they can't be so flexible that people see no reason to abide by them. Thus, you must define them based on your values, and then communicate them clearly and enforce them without exception.

- The other major aspect is setting consequences and then enforcing them. This is what happens when someone attempts to violate your boundaries after you've communicated them. This can be whatever you want; the only thing it cannot be is *nothing*. Failure to do so will create porous boundaries, which are as good as no boundaries at all. However, they also cannot be too rigid.
- Boundaries become important very quickly to enforce, both to assert your rights and defend against those seeking to take advantage of you. Toxic takers are the epitome of those who would seek to take advantage of you, and they come in many forms of selfishness and non-reciprocation.

Chapter 5: Freedom from Yourself

We explored healthy and intelligent ways to put up and enforce boundaries in the previous chapter. A selfish, narcissistic or overly demanding person can jeopardize your serenity and clarity of thought just as much as blatant misinformation or peer pressure. Just as you have boundaries around the quality and content of information you absorb and process, you have boundaries around the people you engage with, the activities you fill your day with, and the lifestyle you choose to lead.

And this brings us neatly to the theme of our final chapter. Lao Tzu said, "knowing others is intelligence; knowing oneself is wisdom." Practice setting boundaries with others, and soon enough, you'll start to wonder – what about behavior that you're unwilling to tolerate *from yourself*? What if the boundary you most need to set up is between a past version of yourself and the present, more evolved version?

The Courage to Change

It's an admirable thing to stand up to toxic takers, get clear on your values and goals, and practice critical thinking and independent thought, despite the social influence and peer pressure. But a nobler goal? Freeing yourself from your past traumas, the demons that haunt you, and the negative beliefs that keep you chained to a limited experience of reality.

Raw intelligence means little if its functioning is constantly colored and clouded by emotions and unconscious issues that cancel out any rational thought you may have. Let's put it plainly: when the past overly influences you, you are less able to think independently, less creative, less adaptable, and less able to think analytically. It sounds like something from an old Kung Fu film, but it's true: in the quest for true wisdom, our most formidable opponent lies within us.

Human beings are storytellers and meaning makers – it's what our brains do. We stitch together a sense of our own persistent identity based on memories and project that identity into the future. Without even knowing we're doing it, we write a script for what life we think we're living, and we play out our role accordingly.

So, what's the problem? As you've seen, the brain that's writing that script is... well, making it up! It's fallible. Self-narratives, personal myths, beliefs, expectations, memories, assumptions, ideas about what is and isn't possible, ideas about who we are... all of these are just *stories*. Just words and symbols. They're nothing more than a brief flicker of electrochemical energy in the brain. True, these stories can be incredibly helpful in organizing our lived experience, but they can also be limiting. Really, really limiting.

Becoming an independent thinker means not taking your word for it, and looking closely at these stories (especially those from the past) to see if they're useful and fit for purpose. You may read a newspaper article and think, "well, this author's bias is pretty obvious!" but when last did you notice the bias in your self-talk? When last did you ask yourself for a citation or supporting evidence before saying something like, "that's just the way I am"?

Picture someone who once weighed 500 pounds but now weighs 100. They've turned their life around completely, yet whenever they walk through a narrow door, they turn their body sideways and walk through carefully, as though they were still 500 pounds. There is nothing wrong with their perception or their brains. They "know" how big they are and how big the door is. The trouble is, they haven't freed themselves from an old set of patterned behaviors lingering on from the past.

For most of us, our past haunts us in less obvious ways, but it's still there, and we are still doing the mental equivalent of turning sideways to fit through metaphorical doors. Here, being an independent thinker means having the courage to change – and that means changing *all the way*, including our attitude to the past and all the old beliefs that were once attached to it.

The Story-teller vs. the Experiencer
Marie is on vacation in a beautiful seaside town, taking in the sights and sounds. At a restaurant, her friends are encouraging her to try the oysters. On autopilot, Marie says, "Oh no, yuck, I never eat seafood, I hate it." Let's take a closer look. At lightning speed and completely unconsciously, Marie has synthesized a series of memories (for example, eating a fish stick at age 5 and throwing up; hearing her mom once say that oysters looked like snot), impressions she's picked up from the media (aren't oysters some cheesy aphrodisiac?) and a long-standing

personal myth she tells herself (called "Marie is a picky eater").

Her friends shrug and enjoy their oysters, Marie orders a burger, and life goes on. The silly thing is, had Marie tasted the oysters that day, she would have discovered something interesting: her narrative was incorrect. There was a whole world of potential oyster deliciousness that she deliberately excluded herself from.

Two things are happening here:

1. There is the real living and breathing Marie, in the present moment, with all her taste buds and neurons firing in her brain, encountering this completely novel experience (or not, in this case).
2. Then there is Marie, who is not inhabiting the present moment but rather living in a story or narrative. This narrative is sometimes based in the past, sometimes the future, but it is definitely, 100% *not* in the present moment.

When Marie is alive and perceiving the present moment, she can be independent of all past assumptions, traumas, old habits and expectations. She is thinking and feeling, and experiencing free from the momentum of the past. When she is in her narrativizing frame of mind, though, she isn't – in fact, she can barely be said to be thinking or feeling or experiencing at all; what she is doing is merely **repeating** the same old story, strengthening it every time until it starts to resemble reality itself for her.

So, we have two choices: we can live life, as it is, here and now, or we can hypnotize ourselves with *stories about* life that take place in the past or future. This oyster example is pretty trivial, but what about the bigger stories we all tell ourselves?

I'll never love anyone else.

It's too late for me to change.

I'm a languages person, my brain just can't handle math.

It's fate, this was supposed to happen.

I have depression, PTSD and sensory issues.

Life doesn't get any better than this.

(Can you hear the Socratic question hidden in each of these... i.e., is this true?)

Of course, walking around life with no persistent sense of self-identity or any narrative at all would be bizarre – like having amnesia. On the other hand, if we were honest, we'd see that a lot of the automatic beliefs and assumptions we have about life and ourselves are limiting us. It is extremely difficult to cultivate free, independent thought when plagued with outdated beliefs and assumptions about yourself.

The storyteller says, "this is happening, now that is happening, I like this, I don't like that, this is bad, this is good…" And while they're churning the same old automatic thoughts round and round, there is one thing they're not doing – experiencing what is occurring, as it's occurring.

Think of these automatic thoughts as though they were your own personalized old wives' tales, rumors and superstitions. People may laugh at the idea that the ancients thought fairies were in the forest, but don't we do the same when we cling to our own tired old preferences and assumptions? Are the personal myths and superstitions we pick up from friends, family, the media or advertising any less silly, when you think about it? Marie "knew" that oysters tasted like snot, without ever having put one in her mouth and experienced it for herself, directly.

So, are you in story-teller mode, or are you living in the real, actual moment, right now?

To think in the present is an art. To recognize when you are influenced by the past (or indeed the future) takes practice and honesty.

Independent thinkers know that genuine, quality, original thought occurs in one place and one place only: RIGHT NOW.

Perceiving the Real

By now, everyone knows about the value of meditation and mindfulness for bringing a busy, wandering mind back to the present. Mindfulness and independent thinking may not seem to have much to do with each other at first, but they are, in fact, natural allies. With mindfulness, we can learn to develop spontaneity, genuine response, and real engagement with the present. We stop defaulting to autopilot mode, or reverting to expectations, assumptions and habits – your own or those inherited from others.

Practicing the fundamentals of independent thought discussed in this book, and cultivating the associated characteristics, cannot be done from inside stale old personal narratives. The present moment is like an eternal laboratory, or an arena where you encounter reality afresh every moment. However, when you get stuck in narrativizing, you're far more likely to be churning around in illusion, distortions, wishes, biases, and ghosts of old memories that were not even accurate the first time around. For example, we can only practice confirmation bias when our story-telling self is in full play, and our curiosity and skepticism take a back seat – after all, they aren't needed if we already know how the story goes, right?

Mindfulness practice is commonly used to help tackle anxiety, but we can also practice experiencing reality without expectations, judgment or assumptions. In other words, meditating can be an antidote to going into autopilot.

A judgment practice

One of the brain's favorite ways to narrativize is to make judgments and assessments.

The moment you make a judgment, you know you are not in the present moment but rather telling a story *about* the present moment. But the now isn't this way or that way – it just is. When we come in with an assessment, rating or value judgment, we muddy our perception and revert to our old mental models, rather than seeing what is in front of us. We lose our independence, as it were, and we also lose curiosity and open-endedness. In our rush to conclude and make definitive pronouncements, we stop perceiving, stop thinking, and instead relax into the comfort of "knowing" (how boring!).

To counter this, try a simple mindfulness practice where you deliberately suspend judgments. To do this, tune into your sense perceptions. The reason for this is simple: your body, and its senses, are always anchored in the present. The mind can wander, but the body is always in the here and now. Tune into the body, and you connect to the now.

1. No need for cushions and incense. Just sit somewhere quiet where you'll be undisturbed, and take a few moments to calm down and become aware of your thoughts.
2. If you have lingering worries or thoughts about what has just happened or what is about to happen, set them aside for the time being – you can come back to them later. Bring your mind to the present.
3. Begin with one sense, for example, sound. Spend a moment sinking into everything you can hear. As you hear, however, notice the tendency to assign labels or judgments (e.g., "that car is annoying" or "I love those birds!"). Imagine you are just encountering the sounds for what they are, as they are. There is no need to label, describe, or call things good or bad. No need for an opinion. Once sensations pass, allow them to pass. Try not to cling to what has come and gone, or wait in anticipation for

what is coming next. Just turn your soft, alert attention to each sensation as it arises in your field of consciousness.
4. If you do make a judgment, that's OK. Notice your judgment, and then *don't make a judgment about it*. Simply perceive your thoughts, including any resistance, without calling it good or bad. Just be curious about what is. Be less interested in giving things names, and just see what they are, right here and now.
5. Move onto the next sense. For sight, explore a single object in close detail. Really, really look at it. For touch, how small a sensation can your fingertips register? Can you see where taste and smell blur together? How many senses can you use to perceive a single object or phenomenon?
6. Play with your sense this way for some time, spending a moment on each. When done, take a deep breath, stretch and come out of your meditation.

When you are an independent thinker, you practice discernment and judgment, and you work extremely hard to separate the wheat from the chaff, intellectually speaking. But all of this should come *after* you've fully perceived and encountered what is in front of you. You want to be a scientist encountering reality with calm, curious neutrality – but even the smartest scientist can spoil their experiments when they make lazy assumptions about what they're looking at!

Before you do anything, first, just become acquainted with *what is*. In your judgments lie a million potential errors. But when you merely perceive, reality can expand in fullness as the thing it is – you may be surprised at just how many solutions and novel perspectives are hiding in the present moment, when you pause long enough to admit that you don't already know everything about it!

You may start to notice when you are in storyteller mode and allow yourself to gently come out of it and simply experience the moment instead. Things you thought you understood inside-out suddenly become new and unknown. Automatic assumptions are shown to be woefully inadequate. Alternatives you never dreamt of start to appear in places you had stopped looking. Not only does life seem a lot more nuanced and interesting than it first seemed, but you start to notice hidden potentials in yourself. Think of all the things that *could* be when you stop insisting on how things *should* be.

You know how some people seem to be "lateral thinkers"? Those creative people who always think outside the box. They possess the clarity of perception that you will be developing with this exercise. Of course, learning to suspend judgment doesn't mean you never make them or that you are completely unwilling to have an opinion or make a claim. It just means that you develop that claim or opinion from an informed position, i.e., a starting point of complete, clear and unbiased attention. This way, your judgments, appraisals and assessments will carry *more* weight and validity. If you stay in your body, and stay with your sensory perception, you stay in the moment. This is an extremely empowering place to be!

The Stoics, ACT and the Power of Value
You are not the same person you were yesterday.

Every day you wake up, you have the opportunity to be different – or better.

The attitudes, beliefs and values that guided you in the past do not necessarily need to guide you now.

All that's needed to grow, learn and evolve is

1. awareness of the fact that you can change and

2. the courage to actually do something else.

That's it. Now, if the above two-part philosophy sounds familiar, it might be because you've encountered it in the classic "serenity prayer" which goes: "God, grant me the serenity to accept the things I cannot change, the courage to change the things I cannot accept, and the wisdom to know the difference." Though this concept is associated with Christianity, its roots are far older, and the sentiment was foundational to many classic Greek philosophies, particularly the Stoics.

Like "cynic" and "skeptic," the word "stoic" has come to have rather different connotations than its original meaning. In the Stoic school of thought, a well-developed human is governed by logic and virtue and lives according to the nature of reality. Self-control over strong emotions, ethical choices and clear, unbiased thinking were considered the keys to a life of value. Practically speaking, this amounted to a personal code much like the serenity prayer suggests: courageously and honestly accept what is true and out of your control, and do your utmost to work on those things that *are* in your realm of control. The art of life is cultivating the wisdom to know when to serenely accept and when to persevere in making changes.

Today, psychotherapists sometimes use a model called Action Commitment Therapy (ACT), which also contains elements of this idea:

1. Using mindfulness practices, become aware of your private emotional experience and life events that are out of your control.
2. **Accept** these for what they are, and make room for them without resistance.
3. Then, **commit to action** driven by your core values to bring about changes that align with the life you want to live.

Acceptance is good. Striving bravely towards a vision you want to create is also good. We can welcome and embrace what is, or we can doggedly try to reshape it according to our vision. *Both* approaches are required for a good life, but skill is needed to know when and how to use each – when to push and when to fall back.

Using this idea in the Stoics, the serenity prayer and in ACT, we can combine mindfulness with conscious, purpose-driven action. This two-step approach helps us fine-tune our discernment and become clear, logical and independent thinkers.

Awareness

Acceptance

Value-driven action

If all of the above are present, our thinking and decision-making processes are turbocharged. We take action that is guided by conscious awareness. We don't waste time fighting what cannot be changed, and instead direct that energy towards those things that most matter to us, which have the greatest chance of enhancing life. We are both rational and purposeful – a powerful combo.

Let's consider a few examples of what this looks like in practice.

Angie has failed an essential module in her final year of university. The news devastates her. Due to a death in the family, financial struggles, *and* having a baby, she couldn't cope with it all and flunked a major exam. Her head is a mess, and for a few days, she descends into self-pitying misery, alternating between rage at herself for allowing it to happen, and blame for all the things that got in her way.

Her student advisor wants to talk – she needs to make some decisions for next year's coursework, and she won't graduate this year. But she is unsure what to do. One moment she feels like doubling down and taking on extra credits so she can finish as quickly as possible, and the next minute she wants to throw the entire degree in the trash and never set foot on campus again. It's the pivotal life moment that many of us face. In this scenario, clear, rational and independent thinking is more crucial than ever – but it's also the least likely to happen by accident.

Let's imagine that Angie is a practiced Stoic philosopher and extremely wise. In such a scenario, here's what she does:

AWARENESS

She takes a day to get still in her mind and tune out all distractions and external pressures. She takes a long walk in nature, meditates a little, then sits down with a journal. She draws three columns: things she can change completely, things she can change somewhat, and things she cannot change at all. She takes a good hour picking apart her difficult situation.

ACCEPTANCE

She takes the column of things she cannot change and physically tears it away and discards it – she cannot change this, so she refuses to spend any more mental energy on it. It's gone. It's over. Her only job in this regard is to accept it. In this column? The fact that she failed. Nothing in the world will help her travel back in time and undo this fact, so she might as well stop railing against it. She is patient with herself, she makes room for any negative feelings this brings up, but she doesn't allow these reactions to control her. She is crystal clear in her mind about this – it cannot be changed, so she will simply not try.

Instead, she commits to focusing on the other two columns. You can probably guess what she puts in the column "things I can change completely." Invariably, this is "my attitude" and "my actions." She dwells on the fact that no matter how bad the situation is, she always has the power to control her reaction to it in the present, her mindset, her thoughts and, most importantly, her actions. Reminding herself that she can take action is a wonderful remedy for feeling powerless about everything she can't change. Even in extremely difficult situations, we have options. They may be limited, or we may not especially like them, but we can always choose – if we become aware that we can choose, that is.

So, how should she act? Go into study overdrive and cram to finish the degree? Leave school completely? Defer until next year? Something else? This is where commitment and values come in. There is a whole universe of possible action open to all of us at any time. *All is permitted, but not all is beneficial.* The thing that will help you determine your course of action is your core values.

COMMITMENT TO VALUED ACTION

Angie takes a moment to clarify this for herself. Above everything, she values her family. She knows this in her bones. Since becoming a mother, her priorities have changed considerably, and she has become aware of this. If she pushes on with extra work, she will only be recreating the same conditions that caused her to fail in the first place. But she doesn't want to drop out entirely either, because she wants to improve her education to earn more and better provide for her family.

Once she clarifies her deepest life purpose and drive, the way forward becomes clearer: she needs to *decrease* her workload going forward, and complete her degree, but only after an additional year. This gives her more time with her family, drops the pressure, and keeps her on track to achieve her dreams.

Seeing this, she knows what is required: patience and persistence. She arranges a meeting with the student advisor and calmly and assertively plans the upcoming year. Notice how her failure – the thing she cannot change – is completely absent from these considerations. She doesn't spend a single second beating herself up or sulking about it. In fact, she feels encouraged and empowered to take action that she knows aligns with what *she* wants for life.

The next time you face a difficult decision or struggle to handle strong emotions, slow down, take a deep breath, and guide yourself through the same process. Independent, calm and rational thought will improve any situation, no matter how dire or complex it seems at first.

Step 1: What am I aware of in this situation, and in myself? Look clearly at the reality in front of you and your feelings, thoughts, and behaviors without judgment. Spend time becoming mindful of as much as you can (you could try a version of the sensory exercise described above). Don't label, interpret, narrativize or make value judgments. Say, "I failed my exam" rather than "I'm a hopeless loser."

Step 2: What is outside of my control here? Your first job is to accept plain facts, which cannot be changed. You don't have to like it; you just have to acknowledge that it is the case. Be honest and brave. Commit to withdrawing your mental and emotional energy from things that cannot be altered.

Step 3: What can I control? What are my options? With curiosity, skepticism, and a mind for evidence, consider possibilities. Acknowledge your emotions, assumptions and bad habits, but don't let them in the driver's seat. Look rationally and calmly at potential action you can take, no matter how small.

Step 4: What are my values? Your life is guided by the compass of your values and your life's purpose. Know this, and the path reveals itself. Do you most value independence? Financial security? Learning? Loyalty? Creativity? Adventure and excitement? Service? Beauty? Love? Your values may change over time, and you may have several competing values.

Step 5: What action can I take towards my values right now? Everything is only theoretical until you take action and make it real. Find the smallest possible action you can take right now to bring you closer to a life lived according to your purpose.

The above process can be done lightning fast: "I missed my train. Oops. Oh well, I can't do anything about that. I'll walk – it's a beautiful evening, and I need the exercise anyway."

If you get into the habit of running through this process, you will notice that it has the power to gently disconnect you from old habits and stale mindsets from the past, and reconnect you to the present moment and your desires within it. You are not the same person you were yesterday, so you should not think or act in the same way as that person.

We always have a choice: we can automatically default to tired old habits (story-telling mode) and do what we've always done, *or* we can choose anew in each moment, using fresh conscious awareness, right now. We can choose to be guided by outdated and limiting mental models, trauma and habit, or we can choose to be guided by logic and clear, well-considered values that give meaning to our lives – and it's *our* life, not anyone else's! *The choice is double: we can choose to have the choice, or we can remain on autopilot, mindless and oblivious to our power to direct our lives.*

Taking Control of a New Narrative
Let's take a closer look at all those things we claimed we wouldn't consider at all: the things we couldn't change. At least by a certain age, most people have several regrets and past mistakes that sit uncomfortably in their memories. If you are evolving as a person, looking back at your past self with

embarrassment, remorse, or even deep shame is basically par for the course!

We can choose to let these moments define us when we work them into our personal narratives and identities. We can feel trapped and condemned by what we've already done, and allow it to change what we feel able to do right now. We can choose to limit or punish ourselves or unconsciously fail to take any further risks out of fear…

Or we can do something entirely different.

We cannot change what has happened, but we can change how we talk about what has happened, the story we tell, and the meaning we ascribe to it. We can choose to learn from past mistakes instead of getting bogged down in negative feelings about them. We can redeem and validate regrets, and transform them into golden opportunities for growth.

Again, as you can see, it all comes down to conscious awareness and the willingness to take proactive control of your life.

You cannot change your past, but you can manage it in the present. Think of events in your history as stars in a constellation. You cannot move the position of any of those stars, but you can change the constellation you draw when you link them up. You can say, "I'm so ashamed that I failed. I was humiliated and felt like an idiot." Or you can say, "I see what I did wrong now. Now, I'm trying something different, so it doesn't happen again."

Have you ever noticed how often people re-christen previous traumatic experiences as valued moments or even blessings after the fact? "Cancer/my divorce/bankruptcy was the best thing that ever happened to me." The event didn't change, but the interpretation did. Some people forgive themselves and move on. Others choose to make the past into an instrument of torture that they punish themselves with, repeatedly. But the past – even the ugly, difficult or confusing parts – can be an unexpected source of energy that can power the life you *do* want to live, right now.

In Angie's case, her massive exam failure may have been a wake-up call to pay more attention to her lifestyle habits, self-care and time management. If she can let go of shame and regret, she might find a few epiphanies and realizations around the event – maybe there's a deeper lesson here if she's willing to learn it?

The past can only be digested and used to enrich the present if it is (you guessed it) accepted and seen for what it is. Then, it can be put to bed. You forgive yourself or others and cut that tie that binds you. As we've seen, being haunted by the past massively impacts your ability to think clearly, logically and independently.

Remember that the past is just a story you tell yourself – and you can tell yourself a different story.

Here's one final exercise that is a fitting end to our book: putting the past to rest by (literally) rewriting it. Sit down quietly with a journal and spend a few moments writing down a paragraph describing a key event that occurred in your past. Don't think too hard about it at first. Now, read back through it and see it for what it is: a narrative.

Can you go back and reword this story? Look at the terms you use, the meaning you inject and the details you pay attention to (as well as those you ignore). Then consciously work to change them according to your current values.

"I was a troubled child" can become "it took me a long time to learn to reign in my natural spiritedness!"

"She dumped me by text" becomes "she lacked the tact I value in a partner."

"It was the scariest thing to ever happen to me" becomes "it turns out I was braver than I thought."

Can you see how perspective is everything? There is a whole universe of possibility waiting in those narrow spaces where interpretations are made. Take conscious control of your own narrative experience. It's both the simplest and most challenging thing you can learn to do for yourself.

If you are interested in this practice, you can further explore cognitive behavioral therapy (CBT) or narrative therapy with a counsellor or psychologist. Or you can go *independently* and experiment on your own... after all, the best experiences are those we create for ourselves.

Summary:

- It's important to find freedom from your past and from the mindsets, attitudes, beliefs and identities that stem from it. If we want genuine change, we need to be courageous enough to redefine what we are, in the present, independent of the past.
- We can operate from "story-teller" mode or "experiencer" mode. The former is where we default to tired old scripts, habits and automatic thinking, but the latter is where we encounter reality directly with no judgments and assumptions – it's the state of

mind where independent, and original thought occurs.

- We can use mindfulness practice to anchor more firmly in the present and experience the real as it is, rather than as we think it is. The body always inhabits the present, and so by using sensory-awareness meditation, we can clarify and focus our perception.
- Try a meditation where you suspend judgment and simply encounter sensory data (on all five senses) without making any pronouncements/value judgments. Countless cognitive errors, biases and distortions occur when we rush in to make judgments, whereas staying open-ended and curious keeps us receptive to solutions, creative alternatives and a genuine appreciation of what is in front of us.
- The Stoics believed that the good life is one lived with emotional restraint, clear thought and adherence to ethics and values. This means having "the serenity to accept what cannot be changed, the courage to change what cannot be accepted, and the wisdom to know the difference." In a more modern manifestation of this principle, Action Commitment Therapy (ACT) also encourages us to **accept** unchangeable conditions of life and commit to taking action according to our **values**.
- Even with the things in life we cannot change, such as past events, we are still in

control of the story we tell. It's worth becoming aware of the language used and the meaning ascribed to past experiences. Then update them to reflect your current focus and values. This has a profoundly empowering effect – and is a hallmark of an independent thinker.

Summary Guide

Introduction

- Independent thinkers can think logically, clearly and autonomously, outside the pressures of their cultures, upbringings, past experiences or historical period. They are conscious and aware, rather than reactive and automatic, and can truly think (and experience) for themselves.
- Cultivating independent thought takes time and effort. The first stage is to assemble a patchwork identity as an independent thinker, and mimic others we see around us. The second stage is to gradually develop trust in our own perceptions and intellectual faculties, while occasionally deferring to convention. The final step is truly independent thought. This free, adventurous, creative, and proactive thought originates purely within us.
- The fundamentals of critical thought include learning to take in information (especially reading) critically, dropping the ego so that you don't get stuck in any one perspective or opinion, having the bravery to be disliked for

being different, and maintaining an open and receptive rather than closed mind. Conventional thinkers differ from independent thinkers in their approach to reality itself, and how they see the function of thinking. For the former, it's to bolster the ego. For the latter, it's for the thrill of encountering reality directly.
- Independent thinking is a way of being that can be practiced and nurtured. We do this by cultivating awareness, dropping ego, and learning to engage critically with the information we take in. This is not the same thing as being a contrarian, who goes against the grain merely to rebel.
- Many famous independent thinkers throughout history shed light on how we might develop the capacity in ourselves. Socrates teaches us the power of asking questions and uncovering our assumptions by taking nothing for granted. Niall Ferguson teaches us about counterfactual thinking, and imagining answers to the question "what if?", and Nietzsche teaches us the value of perspective-switching to enrich our perception of the world.

Chapter 1: Freedom from Illusions of Reality

- Usually, your brain, instincts, gut feelings, emotions, and hunches are all liars (usually).

They aren't doing it on purpose, but they inherently function by jumping to conclusions, saving time, conserving energy, and valuing speed over accuracy. Their goal is to function on less information, and the less of it, the better. Not quite crystal-clear thinking.

- Your feelings and emotions can overpower you and completely color your thinking. But that's confusing feelings for facts. They are entirely separate things. Reality is in fact neutral.

- Your perspective isn't reality. It represents your subjective and unique worldview, but it's not objective, it's not reality, and it is destined to be skewed in terms of your experiences. Some experiences are solidified in what are known as schemas and heuristics, which are the frameworks you use to organize and understand the world.

- Your perception is biased. Understanding the world around you is probably biased because of how the brain jumps to conclusions. These types of jumps are called cognitive biases. They seek to create a story out of as little information as possible, to avoid uncertainty. Battling cognitive biases involves telling stories in reverse, slowing down, and shifting your focus to questions instead of declaratory statements.

- Your memories are wrong. No matter how real and accurate they sometimes feel, a disturbing fact is that memories and false memories end up being indistinguishable to your brain. Factors as small as word choice or pointed questions can distort memories. Unfortunately, we depend on these memories to form our world views and perspectives.

Chapter 2: Freedom from Internal and External Pressures

- An integral part of crystal-clear thinking is to be open-minded. Being open-minded means hearing evidence or an argument and not making an instant judgment. It means being able to say, "I don't know" and resist that feeling of uncertainty. These are all difficult because we are wired to do the opposite.

- The most glaring example of this is confirmation bias, wherein we are deaf and blind to evidence that doesn't support what we think. In other words, we see what we want to see, and we can make a belief appear out of thin air. This is dangerous because it brings the ability to ignore reality. You eventually become entrenched in an echo chamber of reinforcing information that will lead you astray.

- Confirmation bias is also the most prominent way that we fail to simply follow the evidence. If we perform research and keep an open mind, our task is simple: just follow the arrows where they point. But all too often, we are seduced into following the wrong arrows. These include the cognitive distortions of focusing on "must" and "should", black-and-white thinking, the Dunning-Kruger Effect, and labeling.

- The last way we must struggle to keep an open mind and clarity of thought is concerning our social influences. The people around us can determine what we think and do, no matter how hard we try. This was proved in the Asch Conformity Test and the Milgram Shock Experiment. It doesn't matter how open-minded you are; your environment can push you strongly in one way despite your best intentions.

Chapter 3: Freedom from Flawed Thinking

- Practical intelligence is another way of saying common sense, but we all know that common sense truly is not so common. One of the key lessons to learn with practical intelligence is that nothing is what it seems at first glance. The world doesn't readily reveal itself nakedly to you, so it's up to you to look beneath the surface to understand what you see. We want to do this, but we are too often driven by certainty and speed instead of actual truth.

- The first and most natural way to probe below the surface is through cultivating curiosity. There are five types of curiosity, each of which can be a motivation for asking questions: joyous exploration, deprivation sensitivity, stress tolerance, social curiosity, and thrill-seeking. However, curiosity will rarely come easily or naturally, especially about things we don't have an innate interest in. So, we need to generate that same approach through other methods.

- One methodical way to seek truth and simulate curiosity is by embracing skepticism. No, it's not about being *cynical* or simply refusing to believe what people tell you. Rather, it's refusing to blindly believe what people tell you and requiring evidence and facts. In this way, a skeptic is quite similar to a scientist utilizing the scientific method. No answer is required here, and only understanding is sought. Skepticism requires slowing down your thoughts and thinking like a scientist.

- Next, we come to critical thinking. Critical thinking is concerned with questioning answers rather than asking questions. It seeks to take nothing at face value and provide a three-dimensional and nuanced view of a topic or stance. Without that, you are by definition jumping to conclusions or relying on someone else's word—an opinion without inquiry is a weak one. We can practice critical thinking through a series of questions, but we can also go deeper by running inquiries and thoughts through the Paul-Elder framework of critical thinking. This involves three components that ultimately work together to build a bulletproof thinking process: (1) elements of thought and reasoning, (2) intellectual standards to be applied to these elements, and (3) the cultivation and eventual development of intellectual traits.

- Finally, it's important to understand logical arguments—especially *illogical* arguments. This is how you determine the truth and validity of what is being said. We hear these every day but may not pick out their logical flaws. You can think of these as a combination of math and argumentation. There is the conditional statement (X -> Y, true), the converse statement (Y -> X, usually a flaw), the inverse statement (Not X -> Not Y, usually a flaw), and the contrapositive statement (Not Y -> Not X, true). It's not just word games; it's understanding the foundations upon which true and misleading arguments are built.

Chapter 4: Freedom from the Demands of Others

- We tend to think being agreeable and accommodating are positive traits. They are, but only to a certain extent. Studies have shown that too much of either conveys a negative impression to others—precisely what you want to prevent by not asserting yourself. Thus, it seems to make more sense to assert yourself consistently and stop the need for people-pleasing.
- Strong and clear boundaries will be one of your best defenses against people-pleasing and the people who would have you do so. However, they can't exist solely in your head, and they can't be so flexible that people see

no reason to abide by them. Thus, you must define them based on your values, and then communicate them clearly and enforce them without exception.
- The other major aspect is setting consequences and then enforcing them. This is what happens when someone attempts to violate your boundaries after you've communicated them. This can be whatever you want; the only thing it cannot be is *nothing*. Failure to do so will create porous boundaries, which are as good as no boundaries at all. However, they also cannot be too rigid.
- Boundaries become important very quickly to enforce, both to assert your rights and defend against those seeking to take advantage of you. Toxic takers are the epitome of those who would seek to take advantage of you, and they come in many forms of selfishness and non-reciprocation.

Chapter 5: Freedom from Yourself

- It's important to find freedom from your past and from the mindsets, attitudes, beliefs and identities that stem from it. If we want genuine change, we need to be courageous enough to redefine what we are, in the present, independent of the past.

- We can operate from "story-teller" mode or "experiencer" mode. The former is where we default to tired old scripts, habits and automatic thinking, but the latter is where we encounter reality directly with no judgments and assumptions – it's the state of mind where independent, and original thought occurs.
- We can use mindfulness practice to anchor more firmly in the present and experience the real as it is, rather than as we think it is. The body always inhabits the present, and so by using sensory-awareness meditation, we can clarify and focus our perception.
- Try a meditation where you suspend judgment and simply encounter sensory data (on all five senses) without making any pronouncements/value judgments. Countless cognitive errors, biases and distortions occur when we rush in to make judgments, whereas staying open-ended and curious keeps us receptive to solutions, creative alternatives and a genuine appreciation of what is in front of us.
- The Stoics believed that the good life is one lived with emotional restraint, clear thought and adherence to ethics and values. This means having "the serenity to accept what cannot be changed, the courage to change what cannot be accepted, and the wisdom to know the difference." In a more modern manifestation of this principle, Action

Commitment Therapy (ACT) also encourages us to **accept** unchangeable conditions of life and commit to taking action according to our **values**.
- Even with the things in life we cannot change, such as past events, we are still in control of the story we tell. It's worth becoming aware of the language used and the meaning ascribed to past experiences. Then update them to reflect your current focus and values. This has a profoundly empowering effect – and is a hallmark of an independent thinker.

www.ingramcontent.com/pod-product-compliance
Lightning Source LLC
Chambersburg PA
CBHW011129070526
44583CB00023B/2963